ISBN: 9781290455169

Published by:
HardPress Publishing
8345 NW 66TH ST #2561
MIAMI FL 33166-2626

Email: info@hardpress.net
Web: http://www.hardpress.net

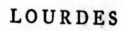

LOURDES

ST. FRANCIS OF ASSISI.

A BIOGRAPHY.

By JOHANNES JÖRGENSEN

Translated from the Danish with
the Author's sanction by T. O'Conor
Sloane, Ph.D.

With Five Illustrations.

8vo, 12s. 6d. net.

—————

LONGMANS, GREEN, AND CO.
London, New York, Bombay, Calcutta & Madras.

BERNADETTE

LOURDES

BY

JOHANNES JÖRGENSEN

*In these lay a great multitude of
sick, of blind, of lame, of withered, waiting for
the moving of the water. And an angel of the
Lord descended at certain times into the pond:
and the water was moved. And he that went
down first into the pond after the motion of the
water, was made whole of whatsoever infirmity
he lay under.*

ST. JOHN v. 3-4.

TRANSLATED WITH THE
AUTHOR'S SANCTION FROM THE ORIGINAL DANISH
BY
INGEBORG LUND

WITH A PREFACE BY
HILAIRE BELLOC

WITH ILLUSTRATIONS

LONGMANS, GREEN, AND CO.
39 PATERNOSTER ROW, LONDON
FOURTH AVENUE & 30TH STREET, NEW YORK
BOMBAY, CALCUTTA, AND MADRAS
1914

PREFACE

IF men would, or could, detach themselves from their own time and place, Lourdes would be the most interesting business in the world.

' Lourdes ' means, of course, the complex of emotion, marvel, site and religious theory, for which that word stands.

Now it is very difficult for men of our time to detach themselves. We are not living in a moment when sheer intellectual force has a social value. Intrigue has the high value it has always had and gains the rewards it has always gained, of shame, accumulated wealth and the contempt of one's fellow-men. Intuitive creative genius still has social value, though it is of less importance in the community than ever before. But intellectual power and the results of an intellectual process have nowadays, for the moment at least, and particularly in this country, no ' market.' I do not mean no market in money, though that is important ; I mean no reward attached to them in fame or respect such that a man will be content to exercise them.

On this account there is always an impediment

opposed to those who would discuss with their fellows in modern England those problems which chiefly exercise the intelligence. One feels it to be beating the air. And to propound matters that demand an intellectual process and the strong grasp of the mind always feels in modern England something like speaking to the deaf in a foreign language—not only to the deaf but to the bored. And speaking to the bored, even if they can make something of what you say, is a very disheartening process.

Nevertheless, such is the driving power of mere truth and the strong appetite of mere curiosity, that men once engaged in an intellectual adventure can hardly refrain from communicating their interest to their fellows. And those who discover what Lourdes means, not to the pilgrim, but to the mere observer who has muscle enough in his mind to detach himself from any modern bias—those, I say, can with difficulty refrain from challenging the attention of their contemporaries to the amazing thing Lourdes is.

Let us present first the popular or newspaper view of Lourdes. Let us next recapitulate in series the known facts about Lourdes. The contrast is almost comic. Lastly, let us judge as soberly as we can what we may say for and against the religious theory about Lourdes based upon these facts.

Well then, the newspaper (which is also the financial) world, the world of the English press in particular, and of such sheets as the *Matin* or the *Tribuna*, and other anti-Christian financial sheets abroad, will have Lourdes to be something after this fashion :—A number

of people belonging to a certain sect called Catholics
(in England the insular term is ' Roman ' Catholics)
frequent a town under the Pyrenees where, under the
influence of very strong emotion, there are produced
certain effects upon them such as strong emotion will
produce : the nervous are less nervous, the stammerer
and the twitched recover control, and in general men
and women under the influence of a violent emotion
discover aptitudes abnormal to their daily powers just
as they will discover such abnormal aptitudes under
any other great strain or shock. This superstition is
commoner with peasants than with townsfolk, and
commoner, of course, with the poor than with the
rich, and with the ignorant than with the cultivated.
Meanwhile it is fostered by those who can profit by it
even at the expense of reason and dignity. The priests
of the sect naturally foster the illusion and accentuate
the abnormal mental conditions of those who come
to be ' cured.' They claim as ' miraculous ' cures
what are often temporary phenomena, and always
phenomena of suggestion.

That is not an unfair summary of the way in which
the kind of people who control our press, and whose
chief concern is the Stock Exchange, desire the mass of
Europeans about them to consider Lourdes. That is
the way they talk about Lourdes, and that is quite
possibly the way they really think about it : for the
men who control our press to-day are as ignorant as
they are brutalised by intrigue and avarice, and
blinded by these and other appetites to reality and to
proportion.

A 3

Now, as against this newspaper legend, let us put a
few facts. I shall be careful not to put them in any
fashion postulating the Catholic Faith. I shall put
down only what posterity will clearly see, whether that
posterity remain Christian and civilised or no. I shall
set down only what academic people call ' objective '
truth : things as they are. In other words, what
ordinary people call ' the truth.'

The truth about Lourdes is simply this. A long
lifetime ago the young daughter of certain poor
parents in the Pyrenean town of Lourdes said that she
had seen in a grotto overlooking the river of that place
a figure. She alone saw this figure, her companions
who were with her did not. The figure was that of a
young and beautiful woman. The figure spoke, proclaiming itself to be Mary, the Mother of that
Personality Whose worship is embodied in a certain
organism known as the Catholic Church; that organism
being in its turn the spiritual aspect and the Form of
European civilisation. In other words, the child
claimed to have had a vision of one of those figures
associated with what is, when they have religion, the
determinant religion of European men. The words
spoken by this vision inculcated repentance, the
frequentation (with the object of a cult) of this grotto,
the drinking of the water which flowed from it and
bathing in the same. Further, the figure said ' I am
the Immaculate Conception.'

There was a great deal more, but I am giving only
the essentials of the story, as a detached but rationalist
historian would present it.

What next followed is exactly what might have been expected. Since this child alone perceived this figure and heard those words it was taken for granted that she was either lying or the victim of an hallucination. But, what is more remarkable, so obvious did this conclusion appear (and it is that which we should all at once have come to upon hearing any similar tale) that even those who could most have profited by making something of the tale were the first to ridicule it. The child's parents, and in particular the priests of religion, the local religious official, and the Bishop of the Diocese himself, thought it unworthy of any other solution.

So far so good : not only history but most private experience is full of things of that kind. But what follows is of a different sort. Certain individuals, willing to test the story or chancing for themselves some cure which they had despaired of, begin to bathe in and to drink those waters. Of those individuals many are cured of their ailments. Time passes. The cures continue and increase in number. These cures have, roughly speaking, only one common feature. They are physical cures, cures of physical ailments. They have NOT in common the feature that the cures so effected are cures of nervous trouble which a strong affection of the mind might reasonably be supposed to promote, at least for a time. Certain of the cures, many of the cures are of this nature. For instance, dumb persons recover their speech, just as dumb persons have often recovered their speech elsewhere under the influence of violent emotion. But then certain other cures, and those exceedingly numerous, are concerned with ailments of a totally different nature—for instance, ulcers. With every passing year the multitude, and what is more remarkable, the *external quality*, of the cures develop. With every year the accumulation of cures admittedly insusceptible to suggestion increases.

We must note this last item in our series of mere facts as a true and plain fact ; a fact like any other, to be admitted by Catholic and non-Catholic alike and a simple piece of contemporary history ; it is evidence no court can refuse, and it is the key to the whole case. With every year the original hypothesis of hallucination, or suggestion, becomes less tenable to the average mind. The average sane visitor to Lourdes who admits miracles in his philosophy, but comes to Lourdes doubtful of phenomena which have been utterly misrepresented in the press, is generally convinced that what he sees at Lourdes is something altogether different from what he had hitherto thought possible or had expected. The average visitor who comes to Lourdes not accepting the miraculous in his system of philosophy has exactly the same experience. Both kinds of men go away either converted or puzzled. Of those who have really and carefully watched the affair in what is sometimes called a ' scientific spirit ' only a very small number remain simply contemptuous and simply postulating a material or even ' psychical ' solution of what they see.

This last fact is exceedingly important. It differentiates Lourdes from all historical parallels to Lourdes.

You can, if you will, deny the great miraculous Christian shrines of the past—Canterbury for instance—because the witnesses to them are dead. The evidence is overwhelming indeed in its amount and detail; but its credibility ultimately depends upon the character of the witnesses—and these are no longer available. The close network of contemporary experience upon which all our judgment of character is built has faded or been obliterated altogether, and you can call the witnesses fools or liars: for they are dead. But you cannot do that about Lourdes. All up and down Europe you will find men still living and submissible to your own judgment, men of the first intelligence and of the widest culture who have visited Lourdes and watched the thing, and who will tell you, if they are at one end of the line that they have seen Heaven open and the power thereof, if they are at the other end of the line that they have been wonderfully puzzled. But you will only find a very few men, and those not usually of the best judgment or of the highest culture, who will tell you that the matter was easily explicable or negligible.

Now when we consider this series of facts let us see what we are to conclude. I do not mean what we are to conclude in the matter of religion, nor even in the transcendental matter, hardly subject to positive proof, of *why* these things arose and What is that which brings them about. I mean only, What is the nature of these things in their relation to us—are they from us or from outside ?

I conceive that by a mere dry process of reasoning

we must determine that there is proceeding at Lourdes
an influence affecting mankind independently of mankind and not proceeding from mankind.

For myself I have come to a much nobler and to a
much happier conclusion, and, from the year 1904,
about Easter time, I have had no doubt that here the
best influence there is for men (I mean that of our
Blessed Lady) is active.   But I am not here concerned
to present a rhetorical or an emotional argument :
only a rational one.

If what happens at Lourdes is the result of self-
suggestion, why cannot men, though exceptionally,
yet in similar great numbers, suggest themselves into
health in Pimlico or the Isle of Man ?   It is no answer
to say that here and there such marvels are to be found.
The point is that men go to Lourdes in every frame of
mind, and are in an astonishing number cured.

Again, it is to be noted that when a definition is
asked, 'Where will you draw the line? What
physical ailment will you say is capable of a cure by
auto-suggestion and what is not ?' those whom you
interrogate are as chary to-day of giving a reply as
they were ready to give it some twenty or thirty years
ago.   They had but to formulate a test for that test
immediately to fail them in the next cure examined.
They had but to say, strong emotion can induce from
within the cure of alpha but not the cure of beta, for
a case of beta and a cure thereof immediately to
appear.

I remember a wealthy and foolish woman saying
some years ago at dinner that she would believe in

miraculous powers if a man who had lost a finger or a
hand by amputation could have it joined again at
Lourdes. To which a priest present at the table
replied, with great judgment, that if or when this kind
of miracle were worked those who still believed the
phenomena of Lourdes to proceed from the cured
themselves would invent a bastard word, half-Greek,
half-Latin, ending in ism and signifying in plain English
the growing together of severed flesh and bone. In
the same way men who now admit that saints in
ecstasy have been raised into the air call that exercise
' levitation.'

But all this is mere reasoning on paper, and that is
not by any means the most convincing process. It is
my advice especially to those who have no devotion or
faith, but whose minds are none the less free and who
have the means and the leisure, to go to Lourdes and
see what they shall see. It is much the greatest
experience in travel they are likely to have in the
modern world.

H. BELLOC.

CONTENTS

ILLUSTRATIONS

LOURDES

I

ON THE WAY—ARRIVAL

It was about four o'clock one morning in June, and a cold grey sky was hanging over the plains of Toulouse. I had left Cette at midnight and had to change at Toulouse—or Tuluze, as the old city, owing its fame to the Troubadours, is called in the soft accent of the South of France—and I expected to arrive at Lourdes at half-past eleven.

True to what I understand to be the reputation of French trains, that in which I was travelling also arrived late. A hurried cup of coffee at the station and then quickly on to the other train. It starts at half-past five ; I contemplate the landscape awhile and am reminded of my own country about Svendborg. On a bridge across the wide Garonne—but soon after I quietly drop off to sleep and do not wake up till nearly eight.

We are still amongst round green hills—or mountains they may perhaps be called now. But the sky is clearing, the chill greyness is yielding to the sunshine. Peasant girls are busy tossing hay in the

B

fields; others, with the black ' capeline '—the Pyrenean head-dress—are strolling slowly towards a village whose pointed church spire soars above the trees. The meadows are filled to overflowing with tall grass and flowers that look very Danish—pink lime-wort, white and yellow ox-eyes, corn-cockle. The embankments are lit up with Our Lady's Candles, perhaps better known as great mullein. The mountains rise to greater heights, ridge beyond ridge. Here and there they are clothed in woods of oak or chestnut. Deep green ravines, the steep roofs of tiny villages clustered round an ancient church. Then comes a view over a hilly and wooded country that reminds one of the Black Forest.

I notice the names of the stations—Tuzaguet, Lannemezan, Lanespède, Lespouey—to me they sound Breton, and very probably they are old Gallic place-names. We stop a long time, far too long, at each of these small stations, with the result that we arrive three quarters of an hour late at Tarbes, the capital of the department to which Lourdes belongs.

At last the train starts again at 11.45—we ought to have been in Lourdes long ago. A flat landscape with rows of poplars passes slowly before the win-dows, far away in a distant haze the mountains—the Pyrenees. Black goats are grazing at the roadside.

Juillan—and far off on a green hill I see a cross! Is it the great cross on Grand Ger above Lourdes?—is that the cross I can see already? A moment later it is gone, hidden by a forest of oaks, and hedges of acacia waving in the wind. The forest recedes; again I look out on flat, green country—the hill with the cross is gone—only far out in the horizon the Pyrenees raise their long, hazy ridges. The sun is shining feebly through the clouds.

At Ossun the clouds gain the day and the rain begins. The mountains draw nearer, advance, close in round the train, looming grey in the mist on both sides.

It is twelve o'clock and the rain is pouring in torrents ; it has evidently been raining a long time in this narrow glen. All the roads bisected by the railway are deep in mud. Through a veil of rain I see wooded hills and beyond them distant mountains shrouded in a monotonous mist.

But now—what do I see ? Is not this the Church of the Pilgrims at Lourdes, the famous Basilica that I know so well from pictures ? Is not that the church I see yonder, on the ridge of a hill that stands halfway into the dale ?—The pointed white spire is outlined against an enormous mountain veiled in mist.

Here is the beginning of a town—orchards, houses, a bridge—a glance at the ' Guide'—no ; it is Adé, it is not Lourdes at all yet ! And the supposed Basilica is simply the parish church——

More fields, more oaks and chestnuts. White cows are grazing on the green slopes. Then for some time we pass through a deep cutting and see only a green embankment on either side. Until a glen spreads out —is it Lourdes ?—Yes ! No ! Yes, it is ! Mist-shrouded hills rise to great heights. . . . There is a factory chimney—houses—and suddenly we are at the platform—Lourdes.

Ambulance vehicles are standing in rows on the asphalt, now bright with the rain, but otherwise there is nothing remarkable to be seen. Only a couple of alert-looking ladies—nurses expecting patients. . . .

I pass the ticket-collector and go through the waiting-room to the hotel omnibus in the great open square where the rain is coming down in torrents. Then into the jolting omnibus and down a steep street. Between the houses a glimpse of the mist-veiled glen —past the market-place where a busy trade is going on under many rain-glistening umbrellas. Down a new street with modern houses, big shops, motor garages. An electric tram-car thunders past. And the omnibus stops between two tubs of laurel bushes, before a *hôtel de luxe*, where gentlemen in swallow-tail coats take possession of my modest luggage and a lady with an elaborate *coiffure* conducts me through long corridors pervaded by the dignified silence of supreme comfort, and shows me rooms at staggering prices. . . .

I select a room as high up as possible, and as a receipt I am accorded the smile suitable to the room and the price. I inscribe my name on the form laid ready for that purpose, stating that I am '*homme de lettres*,' and that I live in Denmark, which information I consider sufficient. Then I am allowed to be alone. From the window there is a view along the foaming Gave, with its rows of poplars, towards the white basilica, whose slender spire is outlined against the background of the lofty mist-veiled mountains.

THE OLD LOURDES—BERNADETTE SOUBIROUS—THE APPARITION OF FEBRUARY 11, 1858

THERE was once, not so very long ago—only fifty years—a Lourdes differing very much from the town that now welcomes visitors and offers them its modern improvements. A humble little country town at the foot of the Pyrenees, only known as a posting station on the road to Cauterets, Barèges, Bagnères, and other watering-places amongst the mountains. There was no railway, but a coach ran from Pau to Luchon, and travellers generally stopped at Lourdes for the midday meal, after which there was just time for a visit to the old fortress frowning from the rock above the town.

Lourdes was a small town, yet not outside the pale of enlightenment. It was the seat of a lower court, consisting of no less than six members ; it had a hospital with its small staff of surgeons ; in the better-class houses might be found *La Revue des Deux Mondes* and *Le Journal des Débats*, while the habitués of the cafés read *Le Siècle*, the little local paper, *Le Lavedan* or *L'Ere Impériale*, published in the adjacent town of Tarbes, where the Prefect of the department resided. Education was provided partly by the municipal schools, partly by religious communities, particularly by the so-called 'Sisters of Nevers.' Many social institutions had continued from the time of the Middle Ages right up to the present day, such as the confraternities into which the working men of the town were organised, each having its own particular chapel in the parish church. There was a guild of Saint Anne for joiners, one of Saint Lucy for tailors, one of Our Lady of Montserrat for masons, one of the Ascension for quarrymen, and so on. The guilds served the purpose partly of the mutual edification of their members, partly of sick benefit societies or burial clubs.

There were corresponding communities for women, the largest one being ' The Congregation of the Children of Mary.' On the whole Lourdes was a pious town and there was, in particular, a fervent love of the Blessed Virgin, and much devotion to her at several shrines in the district, such as Béttharram, Garaison, Piétat, to which the devout paid frequent visits. In the parish church of Lourdes all the altars were dedicated to Our Blessed Lady.

Of course the town was much smaller then than it is now. The whole of it was contained within the small glen which, in a direction from east to west, spreads out to the wider valley formed by the river Gave. On the western side of the valley, and forming a barrier across it, stands the rock crowned by the old fortress said to have been built by the Saracens and to have been the scene of many a fierce contest in the wars of the Middle Ages, from the days of Roland to those of Jeanne d'Arc. The castle hill slopes down abruptly to the green foaming river, and to the south of this hill the main street of Lourdes ended at an old stone bridge across

the Gave and was continued as a road out to the green
meadows along the river side. These meadows were
intersected by various canals through which some of the
water from the Gave made a short cut, instead of going
through the large détour made by the river outside
Lourdes. The largest of these water-courses, Savy's
Canal, flowed into the Gave about three-quarters
of a mile farther down, beneath a projection of the

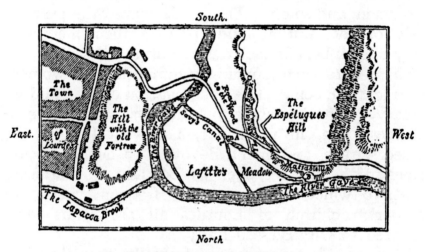

THE DISTRICT ROUND MASSABIEILLE IN 1858.

A = Lafitte's (Savy's) Mill.
B = The Grotto.

Espélugues hill—a steep, bare wall of rock, popularly
known as Massabieille, 'the old rock.' The island
formed by Savy's Canal was called the Châlet, and here
was situated the so-called Lafitte's Mill, which was both
a flour and a saw mill and was the property of a miller
named Savy. The road from Lourdes went farther
south of the canal, across a little brook called Merlasse,
and from there up the Espélugues hill. On the other
hand no road, not even a path, led to Massabieille;

those who wished to go there had either to climb down from the mountain or go through the mill and then wade across Savy's Canal at the end of the Châlet. The country round about Massabieille was always rather deserted, only poor people went there to gather wood for fuel.

And so it happened that three little girls from Lourdes went there on this errand one winter day about fifty years ago. It was on February 11, 1858, at eleven o'clock in the forenoon, and the three little girls were Jeanne Abadie, Toinette Soubirous, and Bernadette Soubirous. Toinette and Bernadette were sisters, Bernadette being the elder, and a little over fourteen years old. She was an ignorant little girl and could neither read nor write ; her parents were so poor that they had been compelled the whole of the previous year, in spite of her delicate health (she suffered from asthma) to let her go out as a shepherdess at Bartrès. She had come back to Lourdes now to prepare for her first communion, but had great difficulty in learning her catechism. She knew, however, how to use her rosary, and always carried it about with her. She did not speak French, but the patois peculiar to Lourdes, and which was more like Spanish.

It was in this patois, her own mother tongue, that Bernadette later on, dozens, nay hundreds, of times, had to repeat the story of what had happened to her at Massabieille on that February afternoon in 1858. This story has been carried all over the world, as far as the Catholic Church extends ; it has been retold by the devout Henri Lasserre as well as by the sceptical Zola. I give the story here in the words in which it

was taken down from Bernadette's own lips by an eye
and ear witness, Jean Baptiste Lestrade, receiver of
taxes in Lourdes in 1858, a man who at first doubted
thoroughly about Bernadette and her story, but who
later became her ardent defender. His book, ' Les
Apparitions de Lourdes, souvenirs intimes d'un
témoin,' was first published in 1899 ; I quote from
a reprint which was issued in Lourdes in 1909.

' It was a Thursday,' Bernadette related, ' and a cold
dark day. After we had finished dinner, mother told
us that there was no more firewood and she was sorry
about it. My sister Toinette and I then offered to
go and gather driftwood along the river-side. My
mother said that she could not let us do that because
the weather was so bad and we might easily fall into
the Gave. Then Jeanne Abadie, who lived next
door, came in, and said she would like to go with us.
She had to take care of her little brother, but she took
him home again and came back a moment after and
said that she had been allowed to go. Mother did not
quite like to let us go, but we begged her, and now that
there were three of us she gave us leave. First we
went out on the road to the cemetery ; firewood is
often unloaded there and you can find sticks and
shavings, but there was nothing that day. Then we
went along the banks of the Gave till we came to the
bridge. We discussed there whether we ought to go
up or down the river. We decided to go down and
went along the road to the woods till we came to
the Merlasse brook. Then we went through Savy's
mill and on to Monsieur de Lafitte's meadows. When
we reached the end of the meadows, almost opposite

the grotto at Massabieille, we were stopped by the canal. There was not much water in it as the mill was not working, but I was afraid of wading across because it was so cold. Jeanne Abadie and my sister were not afraid. They took their sabots in their hands and went over. When they had reached the other side they shouted across to me that the water was very cold, and they stooped down as if to rub their feet to warm them. That made me still more afraid, and I was sure that if I stepped into the water my asthma would come on again. I then asked Jeanne Abadie, who was bigger and stronger than I, to come and carry me over. " No, I am sure I won't," Jeanne answered. " You are a tiresome person to bring out on an errand like this ; if you can't come over by yourself, then stay where you are." ' With this they gathered a few sticks below the grotto, and then disappeared along the river banks.

At this stage of her story Bernadette once or twice mentions a grotto, situated in the rock at Massabieille. In the book referred to above, Estrade thus describes the grotto : 'Massabieille, which faces due north, slopes down steep and sharp like a gigantic wall. But at the base of the rock, and underneath it, there is a cave, about eight yards deep and twelve yards wide and in shape something like a chapel. It is this cave that is called the grotto—the Gave flows close past it—from the river bank to the back of the grotto the ground slopes evenly for a length of fifteen and in a width of twelve yards. One can stand up inside the grotto, and in the vaulting overhead one sees an oblique opening leading to a gallery up above. On one side

MASSABIELLE IN 1858

this gallery ends in a wall of the rock, on the other it opens outwards in a sort of Gothic window, which is half obscured by an immense block of granite. Below this block there is a large, wild rose-bush which hangs down over the rock like a green cascade. . . . Here and there may be seen some plants growing inside the grotto, and in particular a sort of golden saxifrage (*chrysosplenium oppositofolium*) and touch-me-not (balsam).'

Thus far Estrade's description. To return to Bernadette's narrative.

'When they had left me,' she went on, 'I threw some stones into the water so as to step over on them, but it was no use. I then decided to take off my sabots and wade across the canal as Jeanne and my sister had done.

'I had already taken off one of my stockings when I suddenly heard a great noise like a storm coming. I looked to the right and the left, at the trees beside the river, but not a thing moved. Then I thought I must have been mistaken and went on pulling off my stockings, when I heard another noise just like the first. I was frightened then and stood up. I could not shout and did not know what to think, and then I looked across the water at the grotto and saw that a bush in one of the openings was waving about as if it was in a strong wind. Almost at the same time a cloud of a colour like gold came out of the grotto, and soon after a young, beautiful lady, more beautiful than any one I had ever seen, came out and stood in the opening above the bush. She looked straight at me and smiled, and beckoned to me to come over to her as if she had been my mother. I was not frightened any longer, but it was as if I did not know where I was. I rubbed my eyes, I shut them and opened them again, but the lady was still there, smiling and trying to make me understand that I was not dreaming. Without knowing what I was doing I took my rosary out of my pocket and knelt down. The lady nodded as if she was pleased and herself took up a rosary which she carried over her right arm. I was going to begin the rosary and wanted to put my hand up to my forehead to make the Sign of the Cross, but my arm seemed powerless and I could not do it until the lady had crossed herself. The lady let me pray alone, though she let the beads of the rosary glide through her fingers, but she did not say anything. Only, at the end of each decade, she said with me, " Glory be to the Father, and to the Son, and to the Holy Ghost."

' When the rosary was said the lady withdrew into the back of the grotto and the golden cloud disappeared with her. As soon as the lady was gone Jeanne Abadie and my sister came back to the grotto and found me kneeling. They laughed at me for my devoutness and asked me if I was coming home with them or not. I waded through the brook without any trouble now and the water seemed to me to be lukewarm—like water for washing dishes.

' " That was nothing to make such a fuss about," I said to Jeanne and Toinette as I dried my feet ; " the water isn't cold at all, as you would have had me believe."

' Then we tied up three bundles of the branches and driftwood that the others had gathered ; we went up the side of Massabieille and so reached the road to the wood. As we were going back to the town I asked Jeanne and Toinette if they had not noticed anything at the grotto.

' " No," they said. " Why do you ask ? "

' " Oh, never mind. It does not matter."

' All the same I could not help telling my sister about the strange thing that had happened to me at the grotto, but I asked her not to tell anyone about it. All that day I thought of the lady, and in the evening, when we were all saying our prayers, I began to cry. Mother asked what was the matter, and Toinette hurried and answered for me, so I had to tell her myself what had happened. The others asked me what the lady had looked like. I said that she looked like a young girl of sixteen or seventeen. She was wearing a white gown with a blue girdle, the ends hanging down on one side. On her head she had a white veil so that you could hardly see her hair, and at the back the veil fell below her waist. Her feet were bare, but the folds of her gown almost covered them except quite in front, and there was a golden rose on each. On her right arm she had a rosary of milk-white beads, joined together with golden links that shone like the two roses on her feet.

' " It is all something you have imagined," Mother said. " You must put those fancies out of your head. And you must not go to Massabieille any more ! "

' Then we went to bed, but I could not sleep. All the time I saw the sweet, lovely lady before me, and, no matter what my mother had said, I could not believe that I had been mistaken.'

III

THREE MORE APPARITIONS

UP to this time Bernadette had been like most other children. The ' Sisters of Nevers,' whose school she attended, had not noticed anything remarkable about her. When not prevented by her asthma she played about in the garden like the other scholars. As a rule she was cheerful, even gay, with the simple gaiety of a child. There was no morbid religious excitement about her. She was preparing for her first Communion at this time, but the priest who had her under instruction, in a class with other children, did not even know her. Later on, when her visions began to be talked about, he called her up at one of his lessons to question her, merely in order to see her. A shy and poorly-dressed little girl came forward, and it was evident to the priest that she was very simple-minded and ignorant. Her confessor, the Abbé Pomian, said later, ' There was nothing in the least remarkable about Bernadette. She was ignorant and her intelligence was below the average.' Some time after, when she entered a convent, the Superior said of her : ' She is good, but there is no exaltation, not even any enthusiasm in her.'

Another account from the year 1869 [1] says, ' Berna-

---

[1] *Annales de la Grotte*, vol. ii. April 30.

dette was good, gentle, straightforward, simple ; her piety was edifying but not astonishing. Her mind had no suppleness, her imagination no variety. . . . She had no gift of vivid or interesting description ; when speaking about her vision, her manner of narration was concise, colourless, and cold ; one had to question her again and again in order to get a complete account. She spoke without any sign of inner emotion ; after a while she might be carried away by her subject, but there was never any ardour about her manner. . . . She was really insignificant.'

It is necessary to emphasise all this in order to ward off the obvious explanation that Bernadette was a hysterical or religiously excited little girl. She was not, either at this time or ever afterwards. The whole of her spiritual life was healthy, normal, and quite average.

But after that 11th of February it seemed to Bernadette's mother that her little girl was not the same as before. There was something strange about her—a look of sadness—and a yearning after Massabieille, where she had seen the beautiful apparition that she could not help longing to see again. A day or two passed by—Friday, Saturday—and on Sunday afternoon Bernadette's mother could not bear any longer to see her favourite child drooping and sad. The three children therefore, this time accompanied by quite a little troop of friends who had been admitted into the secret, again directed their steps to the grotto beside the foaming Gave. Bernadette's mother had given them a bottle of holy water, of which they were to sprinkle a few drops in the direction of the vision, lest it should be anything from an evil source. . . .

On the way out the little company divided into
two parts, the first being led by Bernadette and the
second by her friend, Jeanne Abadie. They did not
go by way of the Châlet, but chose the straight road
across the Merlasse brook to Massabieille, in order
to climb down the rock to the grotto. As soon as
Bernadette had reached the goal of her walk she
knelt down and began to pray, with her eyes turned
towards the window-shaped niche in which the lady
had first appeared. The others did not pray with her,
but suddenly they heard their little playmate exclaim,
' There she is, there she is ! '

One of them, who was at this moment holding
the bottle of holy water, quickly handed it to Bernadette and said, ' Quick, throw the water at her ! '

Bernadette seized the bottle and flung the contents
out in the direction of the rose-bush.

' The lady is not at all vexed about it,' she declared ;
' quite the opposite, she is nodding and smiling at us.'

At these words the other little girls knelt down and
arranged themselves in a semicircle about Bernadette.
She did not seem, however, to notice them any more.
Her glance rested steadfastly and with a look of the
most intense joy on the grotto, where none of the others
saw anything but the bare rock and the leafless bush.
Bernadette's face was radiant, her usually rather
commonplace, though pretty, features seemed to be
transfigured by some inner light ; the children gazed
at her and could not recognise her. Quite over-
whelmed they began to cry, and one of them exclaimed,
' I hope Bernadette isn't going to die ! '

At the same moment a stone was thrown down
from the heights above, and this sudden rolling and

rattling noise was enough to make all the girls start up and rush off screaming in all directions. They were, however, soon assembled again, when they found that it was only Jeanne Abadie who was on the road above and wanted to frighten them, and who now with her friends stood and laughed heartily at them. Then they all went down to Bernadette and found her immovable, in the same state of ecstasy as before. The little girls did not know what to do with her, and in their distress they ran to Savy's mill for help. The miller's wife and her son both came back with them ; the latter, a young man of twenty-eight, carried Bernadette, still rigid and unconscious, to the mill, where she at last came to herself.

In answer to their questions Bernadette told the mill people that she had seen, in the main, the same vision as on the Thursday. In the meantime her mother had been sent for and now arrived, full of indignation at the long time the children had stayed away and at what she called Bernadette's nonsense.

'Do you mean to make us the laughing-stock of the whole town ? ' she shouted to her daughter as she was coming to the house. She threatened the child with a substantial stick, and it was only with difficulty that the miller's wife rescued Bernadette from making a closer acquaintance with it. At last, with tears of annoyance and vexation, Madame Soubirous took her child home. There was to be no more going to Massabieille now !

Again some days passed. Bernadette went to school and did not talk any more about ' the lady.' But others in Lourdes talked the more, and on Wednesday evening, February 17, two devout ladies,

c

Mademoiselle Antoinette Peyret and Madame Millet, paid a visit at the house of the Soubirous in order to hear a little more. They came in just as Bernadette had plucked up courage and again asked her mother if she might go to Massabieille. Thanks to these ladies, who promised to go with the child and take care of her, the permission was given. And on the morning of February 18, before daybreak, the little company of three walked along the road, already so dear and so familiar to Bernadette, to the grotto. Arrived there, the two ladies lit a blessed candle which they had brought with them and all three knelt down and began to pray. It was not long before Bernadette uttered a cry of joy :

'She is coming ! There she is ! '

And trembling for very joy she bent her head close to the ground in greeting to the glorious visitant.

The two ladies saw nothing. They saw only the joy in Bernadette's eyes and in her quiet, happy smile. But the little seer did not fall into an ecstasy this time, and Mademoiselle Peyret, who had naïvely brought pen, ink, and paper, handed all three to Bernadette with the words : ' Ask the lady, if she has anything to say to us, to write it down ! ' Bernadette took what was given her and went the few steps up from the place where she had been kneeling, to the grotto of the apparition. Standing on tip-toe she held up the writing materials towards the mysterious figure. She stood for a few moments like this, looking up and—so it seemed—listening to something that was being said to her. Then she let her arms drop to her side, made a deep obeisance, and went back to her place.

'The lady smiled when I held up the pen and ink,' she said, 'but she was not vexed and she gave me an answer. She said, "What I have to tell you I do not need to write." And then she added,[1] " Will you do me the favour to come here every day for two weeks ?'

'And what did you answer ?' asked Mademoiselle Peyret.

'I promised to come.'

'But why did the lady want you to come ? '

'I don't know. She did not say anything about it.'

Bernadette and her two companions then resumed their prayers. The two ladies noticed that the little seer often ceased her rosary prayers and seemed to engage in an interior conversation with one who was invisible to them. This lasted for about an hour, then Bernadette declared that the apparition had vanished.

'And did she not say anything more to you ? ' the ladies asked her, on the way home.

'Yes,' answered Bernadette, in a tone of mingled joy and sadness; 'she said, " I do not promise to make you happy in this world, but in the next."'

'If the lady talks to you like that, why don't you ask her to tell you her name ?'

'I have asked her.'

'And who is she, then ? '

'I don't know. When I ask her she only smiles and bends her head.'

---

[1] According to Estrade's account, for the word 'favour ' Bernadette sometimes used the expression ' *boulentat* ' (*bonté*), sometimes ' *gracia*.'

By this time Bernadette and the two ladies had reached Lourdes, and the latter accompanied the little seer to the humble cottage of the Soubirous in the Rue des Petits Fossés—a steep winding lane in the oldest part of the town, crouching beneath the old fortress and dominated by its threatening towers and battlements, and dreary empty window spaces.

Bernadette now told her mother about the promise she had made to the lady. The good woman did not know what to do, and at last went to ask advice of her older sister, Bernarde. The sister wanted time for consideration, but later in the day came down to the Rue des Petits Fossés, and gave it as her opinion that for once Bernadette ought to be allowed to go out to Massabieille, but that her mother ought to go with her. Next morning, therefore, Bernadette, in company with her mother and her aunt, set out for the grotto, about half a dozen women following them at some distance.

Arrived at Massabieille, Bernadette at once knelt down, took out her rosary, crossed herself and began to pray. A moment after the world about her no longer existed for her, the vision had appeared and she was in an ecstasy. Her face was transfigured, her slender little figure was bent forward, it seemed as though she must be lifted up bodily to the object of her gaze. Without knowing why, all the women about Bernadette were seized with trembling, and her mother exclaimed involuntarily, ' Oh, my God, do not take my child from me ! ' Their eyes were dimmed with tears, and they all prayed silently and earnestly. Bernadette's ecstasy lasted half an hour. Then it seemed as if she awoke, she rubbed her eyes, rose from her knees and came, still radiant with happiness, to her mother and aunt, who took her in their arms without a word. Questioned as to what the lady had said, Bernadette answered that she had said she was pleased at her having come, and promised to tell her important things on a later occasion.

And so began the fourteen days on which Bernadette every morning went to the grotto, the days from February 18 to March 4.

IV

A DOCTOR'S OBSERVATIONS—THE ATTITUDE OF THE
CIVIL AUTHORITIES

Le Lavedan, the local paper at Lourdes, in its issue of
February 20, 1858, contained an article briefly reporting
the events which were the general subject of discussion
in the town.   After the report it continued :

'A thousand explanations have been forthcoming,
but these we do not wish to discuss.   We will only
say that the young girl goes out to the grotto every
morning to pray, with a lighted candle in her hand, and
accompanied by over five hundred persons.   She is
seen first to fall into a state of devout reverence, then
she smiles gently and is rapt in ecstasy.   The tears
stream down her cheeks and her eyes are steadfastly
fixed on that place in the grotto where she believes
she sees the Blessed Virgin.

'We promise to keep our readers informed of this
extraordinary movement, which is daily gaining more
adherents.'

Le Lavedan was right in its statement about the
numbers of people who had joined Bernadette in her
daily pilgrimage to Massabieille.   On the second of the
fourteen days, that is, on February 20, there were
really hundreds of people in front of the grotto.   The

large crowds did not, however, seem to embarrass Bernadette. It was as though she did not see them—they did not make her shy, but on the other hand she made no display of herself before them. She knelt down, took out her beads and began to pray, quite as if she had been alone, or with only her mother and aunt near her. And she had scarcely been more than a minute at prayer before her face was enkindled with a radiance like that which shone from Moses when he came down from Sinai. Madame Soubirous burst into tears and exclaimed, ' Is this my daughter ? Is this Bernadette ? I can't recognise her at all ! '

Then came February 21, which this year fell on a Sunday, the first Sunday in Lent. Before sunrise a concourse of several thousands of people was already gathered about the grotto and in the meadows on the other side of Savy's Canal. Bernadette came as usual, quietly and modestly, her white *capeline* on her head and her kerchief knotted on her breast, accompanied by one of her relatives.

One of the spectators that morning was a doctor in Lourdes, a Doctor Dozous, who was permeated through and through with the sceptical rationalism of the France of that time. He has himself told, in his book, ' La Grotte de Lourdes, sa fontaine, ses guèrisons,' the impression made upon him by what he saw.

' As soon as Bernadette reached her place opposite the grotto she knelt down, took out her rosary and began to pray, letting the beads glide through her fingers. Her face underwent a change which was noticed by all the persons near her, and which indicated that she was *en rapport* with her vision. While she let the beads glide through her left hand, she held in her right a lighted candle. The wind being strong that morning the flame often went out, and each time this happened she held out the candle to the person nearest her, to have it lit again.

' As I was anxious to know how this state affected her circulation and breathing, I took hold of her arm and felt her pulse. It was quiet and normal, her breathing too was regular ; there was no indication of nervous excitement.

' After I had taken my hand from her arm Bernadette arose and went a little nearer to the grotto. Soon after this I saw her face, which up to now had been radiant with the utmost happiness, assume a look of sadness. Tears were running down her cheeks. I wondered very much at this change, and when she had finished her prayers and the mysterious vision had disappeared, I asked her the reason. She answered : " The lady turned her eyes from me for a short while and looked out over my head. Then she looked at me again, and when I asked why she looked so sad she said, " Pray for sinners."

' Then Bernadette left, as modestly and quietly as she had come.'

So far Dr. Dozous. During the course of the Sunday he would probably have occasion to discuss the matter with other people of some standing in the town. Lourdes was, in fact, wholly taken up with Bernadette and her visions and could talk of nothing else, and it was to be expected that the crowds would increase daily.

It was no wonder, then, that the public authorities

in Lourdes found it necessary to interfere and keep order, and that the mayor, the imperial procurator and the commissary of police already that very Sunday met together in the town hall in order to make the necessary arrangements.

In the morning, as Bernadette was coming home from church, a policeman came up to her and asked her, in the name of the law, to come with him.

Bernadette was brought before the *procureur impérial*, Monsieur Dutour, the chief judge in Lourdes.

' My dear child,' he began kindly, ' you are being talked about a good deal of late. Do you intend to keep on with your visits to that grotto ? '

' Yes, monsieur. I have promised the lady to come. I have still twelve times to go.'

' But, my little friend, that lady does not exist at all. It is only something you imagine.'

' Yes, I thought so too, at first. I rubbed my eyes because I thought I was dreaming. But I know now that it is no dream.'

' How do you know that ? '

' Because I have seen her several times. The last time was this morning. And she speaks to me, too.'

' But the Sisters at the school you go to—they say, too, that it is all imagination.

' The Sisters would not say that if they saw the lady as plainly as I do.'

' Take care, my dear, perhaps it won't be long before we find out something that will explain why you are so obstinate. There are people who say that you and your parents receive money for it secretly.'

' We receive nothing from anybody.'

' Anyhow, your behaviour at the grotto is a perfect

scandal. You fool people into going there. There must be an end to it. Will you promise me not to go to Massabieille any more ? '

' I can't promise that, sir.'

' And is that your last word ? '

' Yes, sir.'

' Very well then, you may go. You will hear from me later.'

The imperial procurator made no secret of the fact that he had not been able to manage Bernadette, and that afternoon at the club he related the whole of his interview with her. Monsieur Jacomet, the commissary of police, perhaps inspired by this account, resolved to settle the question, and the very same day, towards evening, he sent for Bernadette. The interview took place in the presence of Estrade, who lived in the same house, and who could therefore, as if by chance, come into the office while Bernadette was there. Just like Dutour and Jacomet, Estrade also thought that it was a case either of a morbid imagination or of conscious fraud. In his book he says :

' The child who here stood before me, and whom I saw for the first time, seemed to be about ten or eleven years old, though she was actually fourteen. Her complexion was clear and healthy, her eyes suggested a character of great gentleness and simplicity ; her voice was a little too strident, yet still pleasant. I did not notice ,her asthma. She sat down opposite M. Jacomet's desk in an unconstrained attitude, with her hands folded on her knees and her head slightly bent. She was wearing a white *capeline* ; the rest of her dress was plain but clean and neat.'

Just as Estrade came in M. Jacomet was saying, in his friendliest manner :

' No doubt you have already understood why I have sent for you ? I have heard so much about all the beautiful things you see at Massabieille that, like everybody else, I should like to hear more. Would you mind telling Monsieur Estrade and myself how you made the acquaintance of the lady in the grotto ? '

' No, sir.'

' Your name is Bernadette, is it not ? '

' Yes, sir.'

' And your surname ? '

The child hesitated a moment. Then she said, ' My name is Bernadette Soubirous.'

' How old are you ? '

' Fourteen.'

' Aren't you making a mistake ? ' asked the commissary, with a smile.

' No, sir, I am not. I am fourteen past.'

' And what do you do at home ? '

' Not very much, sir. Since I came home from Bartrès I have been going to school to learn my catechism. After school I look after my little brothers and sisters.'

' So you have been to Bartrès. What did you do there ? '

' I stayed for a few months with my foster-mother. She set me to mind the sheep.'

With various questions of this kind Jacomet put Bernadette at her ease. Then all at once he said :

' And now, my child, we come to that which I want you to tell me about ; that is, what it is that has made such an impression on you at Massabieille. You need not be afraid. Just tell me everything.'

Bernadette needed no persuasion now, and told him all about her first vision, such as it has been told here. She gave all the details about the lady's age, her clothes, appearance, all with such a convinced *naïveté* that it was impossible to doubt her sincerity. While she was speaking the commissary quickly jotted down some notes in pencil. At last he looked up and said :

' All that you have been telling me just now is very interesting. But who *is* this lady that you have taken such a fancy to ? Do you know her ? '

' No, I don't know her.'

' You say she is very beautiful. Is she like anybody you know ? '

' Oh, sir, she is much more beautiful than anyone I have ever seen.'

' She can't be more beautiful than, for instance, Madame X—— or Madame U——? ' Jacomet mentioned two ladies who were acknowledged beauties in Lourdes.

' They can't be compared to her ! '

' Can this lady move about, or is she immovable like the statues in the church ? '

' Oh no, she moves about, and smiles and speaks like anybody else. She has asked me to do her the favour of coming out to the grotto every day for a fortnight.'

' And what did you say to that ? '

' I promised to come.'

' And what do your father and mother say to all this ? '

' At first they said it was all imagination—— '

' Yes, my dear, and they were right—— ' Jacomet interrupted with sudden gravity. ' All this, that you believe you see and hear, only exists in your own imagination.'

' Other people have said that too, but I am quite certain that I am not mistaken.'

' Now listen to me, Bernadette. If that lady in the cave was a creature like the rest of us, then everybody ought to be able to see her and hear her. How can it be, then, that this is not the case ? '

' I can't explain that, sir. I can only say that the lady is real and alive.'

' Well, if you will insist on it, then believe what you like, for all I care. But as it is not unlikely that the Prefect will have to take up the matter, you must tell me if I have understood you rightly.'

With this Jacomet took up the paper on which he had made his notes and read them out, purposely making some alterations in order to confuse Bernadette.

' You said that the lady seemed to be between seventeen and twenty years old ? '

' No, I said between sixteen and seventeen.'

' And that she was wearing a blue gown with a white girdle.'

' No, it was the other way about : a white gown with a blue girdle.'

' And that her hair fell down her back.'

' No, it was her veil, not her hair.'

Bernadette was not self-assertive in making these corrections ; nor, on the other hand, was she timid.

Jacomet understood that he would not succeed in entrapping her into contradicting herself. He changed his tactics. Looking straight at the young girl he said :

' My dear Bernadette, I have asked you to tell me your little story yourself, but I must confess that I knew it beforehand. I knew it—and I know who has taught it you.'

Bernadette met the commissary's look as she answered :

' I don't understand what you mean.'

' Then I will explain. Now tell me honestly, is there nobody who has set you to go about and tell people that the Blessed Virgin has appeared to you at Massabieille, and that if you only did this you would be looked up to as a great saint, and that the Blessed Virgin would be pleased? Take good care how you answer, I know more than you perhaps think.'

' There is nobody, sir, who has told me to do that.'

' Very well. I know what I know. I won't question you further. But in return promise me one thing, that vou won't go to Massabieille any more.'

' I have promised the lady to go.'

' Oh, have you indeed!' the commissary cried, as he jumped up from his chair and pretended to be angry. ' So that is your way, is it? You think you can make fools of us all with your stories and your stubbornness? No, my dear; and if you don't promise me at once, this very instant, that you will never go out to Massabieille again, I will call a policeman, and then you will be put into jail!'

Bernadette did not answer. At this point Estrade judged it right to interfere and approached the little seer. 'My dear child,' he said, 'don't be so obstinate. Say yes to what M. Jacomet asks of you. It is for your own good.' But Bernadette did not answer him either, and perhaps the matter would have ended there if her father, François Soubirous, had not come in just then to fetch his daughter.'

'Master Soubirous,' exclaimed Jacomet, 'you come just at the right moment! You know the part your daughter has taken upon herself to play lately. There must be an end of these monkey tricks that are turning the town upside down. So if you have not the necessary authority to keep your daughter at home, then I must see about keeping her out of mischief elsewhere.'

Bernadette's father, a poor, bankrupt miller, who earned only a bare subsistence as a day labourer and who had a wife and six children to keep, promised, after a feeble protest, to do what the authorities required. On the way home, he said to his daughter:
'My dear little Bernadette, you don't want to get us all into trouble, do you? All the great people in the town object to your going to that grotto—you will really have to give it up.'
'Father,' said Bernadette, 'I can't help it. It is as if there was something inside me calling and drawing me, so that I *must* go.'
'However that may be,' answered François Soubirous, 'I forbid you to go, and you won't disobey me, will you, for the first time in your life?'
'No, father, if you wish it, I will do my very best to struggle against going.'

V

THE APPARITIONS ON THE 23RD, 24TH, AND 25TH FEBRUARY—THE FOUNTAIN

NEXT morning, therefore, Bernadette did not go to the grotto. She was at school in the forenoon, ran home at twelve for dinner, and then set out again to go to the convent. But suddenly, as she was walking along the street, she felt as if she was stopped by an invisible barrier. It was as though she found herself in front of a wall through which she could not pass. She turned to the right, tried to go to the left ; the wall was everywhere, right across the street. Then Bernadette understood, or thought she understood. Quickly she turned round and was soon at the grotto, where a large number of people had assembled. Bernadette said her prayers as usual, but the lady did not appear. A couple of *gendarmes* had followed Bernadette, and some facetious persons would have it that ' the lady ' had been afraid of them. Madame Soubirous arrived on the scene, greatly distressed at the disobedience of her child. Several people there, however, spoke very warmly in defence of Bernadette, and her mother at last promised not to prevent the child any more from going to Massabieille.

Accordingly on the 23rd she went out as usual in the morning, amongst the spectators that day being the

tax receiver, Estrade, who had come for the first
time, chiefly to comply with the request of his sister.
Subjoined is his own account of what took place that
morning :

'In company with the three ladies, for a couple
of friends had joined my sister, I arrived at Massabieille
at about six o'clock, just at daybreak. On the way
out and going through the town, I had felt somewhat annoyed at having to walk in such a large procession, and I now tried to look as supercilious and
indifferent as possible. The seer had not yet arrived,
but from a hundred and fifty to two hundred people
were already assembled. I was glad to see amongst
them three or four gentlemen from Lourdes ; if I am
not mistaken they were Dr. Dozous, the advocate
Dufo, the commandant at the fortress, and Monsieur de Lafitte. Otherwise the gathering was composed chiefly of women, who were praying with an
earnestness worthy of a better cause.
'After we had waited a few minutes, there was
a murmur through the crowd—people made way—
Bernadette was coming. The other gentlemen and
I pushed our way forward to the front rank so that
we could get a good view of the young girl.
'Bernadette knelt down, took out her rosary,
and made a deep reverence. She was not embarrassed,
but, on the other hand, she did not make any display
of herself. Her behaviour was quite natural, as if
she had been in church at an ordinary service. While
she let the first beads of the rosary glide through
her fingers, she looked with expectant eyes at the
rock—a look that showed how impatiently she was

D

waiting. And all at once it seemed as though she gave a start of admiration, it was as if she were born anew. Her eyes lit up and shone, an angelic smile played about her lips ; her whole figure became extraordinarily graceful. She looked as though her soul were striving to burst the bonds of its corporeal sheath and proclaim its joy to all the world. Bernadette had ceased to be Bernadette. . . .

' After the first rapture caused by the appearance of the lady was over, one could see that she became attentive and that she was listening. Her gestures, her expression, everything showed that someone was speaking to her. Now she smiled, now she looked grave ; she bent her head in assent, or she seemed to ask a question. When the lady spoke to her a shiver of joy seemed to pass through her ; at other times she seemed to ask for something and her eyes filled with tears. Now and then the conversation seemed to have ceased. Bernadette again began to use her beads, but always with her eyes on the rock. . .

' Usually Bernadette finished her prayer with a salutation to the invisible lady. I have been much in society, but I have never seen anyone make so graceful or distinguished a salutation as Bernadette. During her ecstasy she now and then made the Sign of the Cross. As I said that morning on the way home, if the blessed in Heaven make the Sign of the Cross, they must do it in that way.

' The ecstasy lasted about an hour. Towards the end the seer moved, still on her knees, from the place where she had been praying close up to the rose-bush that hung down from the rock. There she kissed the ground and then returned, still in a kneeling position, to her starting-point. A last radiance passed over her face ; then the rapture faded from it, little by little, almost imperceptibly, growing paler and paler till it had quite disappeared. The young girl continued praying a while yet, but it was only the pretty, rustic-looking little Bernadette Soubirous. At last she stood up, went over to her mother and disappeared in the crowd.'

Estrade did not go next morning to the grotto. His sister, however, was present in the constantly increasing crowd, strangers from other towns in the district having now added to its numbers. From the account that she gave her brother, the events were about the same as on the day before, except that Bernadette, after she had kissed the ground under the rose-bush, turned round to those present, and, with a face swollen with weeping and her voice choked with tears, exclaimed, ' Penance, penance, penance ! '

We now come to the 25th of February, the day when the wonder-working fountain, which has made Lourdes famous, gushed forth for the first time. Here again I avail myself of Estrade's version :

' After a few minutes of quiet prayer,' he says, ' Bernadette arose and went towards the grotto. She turned aside the overhanging branches of the rose-bush and kissed the ground underneath the ledge of rock, behind the bush. Then she came back and again became rapt in ecstasy.

' She had said perhaps two or three decades of the rosary[1] when she again arose and seemed to be

[1] This consists, as is well known, of five decades. Each decade consists of one large bead and ten smaller ones. An ' Our Father ' is said at each of the large beads, and a ' Hail Mary ' at each of the smaller ones, and each decade concludes with a ' Glory be to the Father, and to the Son, and to the Holy Ghost.'

perplexed. First she turned to the river and went two or three steps in that direction. Then she suddenly stopped, looked back as if some one had called her, and stood listening, after which she nodded and again went forward, this time to the grotto, towards the left corner of it. Having gone three-fourths of the way she stopped again and looked hesitatingly about her. She looked up as if to ask a question of the lady; then she stooped down and resolutely set to work to scratch up the ground. The small hollow she had thus made quickly filled with water, and after having waited a minute or so she drank of the water and washed her face in it. She also took some grass growing in this place and put it in her mouth. All the onlookers watched these movements with the greatest consternation and a sense of something eerie. When Bernadette at length arose and showed a face quite dirty with the muddy water, all exclaimed as if with one voice, in a tone of horror, " Bernadette has gone out of her mind ! "

' Bernadette herself did not seem to notice anything. Some one dried her face and it shone as before. But no one admired her now, only pity was left, and disappointment filled all hearts. Somewhat ashamed and crestfallen, people slunk away and Bernadette was left almost alone.'

Estrade was amongst those who left. Bernadette's ecstasy was not over until about seven o'clock. Then the faithful few who had remained behind asked her, ' But, Bernadette, what made you do such strange things this morning ? Why did you go here and

there ? Why did you scratch up the soil ? Why did
you drink of the muddy water ? '

Bernadette answered : ' While I was praying the
lady said to me, kindly but gravely, " Go along to
the spring, drink of the water and wash yourself in it."
As I knew nothing about any spring I thought the
lady meant the river and went in that direction.
But the lady called me back and pointed to the grotto.
I did not see any water there, and as I did not know
what else to do, I scratched up the soil and then the
water came. I let it run a little clearer first, then I
drank of it and washed myself in it.'

' But you ate some of the grass, too, beside the
spring ; why did you do that ? '

' I don't know. I felt inwardly that the lady
wanted me to do it.'

There could be no doubt that Bernadette had
found a spring. People who came out to the grotto
in the afternoon noticed the little stream which had
already channelled a course for itself in the ground
on its way down to the river Gave. The report of
it soon spread in Lourdes and next morning the
gathering at Massabieille was larger than ever. People
did not only want to see Bernadette, they wanted
above all to see the spring. The Pyrenees are rich in
mineral springs ; and there is a whole circle of mineral
watering-places about Lourdes—Cauterets, Barèges,
Luz, Saint-Sauveur. All sorts of hopes and expecta-
tions, therefore, were immediately centred in this
wonderfully created stream.

The numerous spectators saw the spring in full
activity on the morning of February 26. It had
already grown to the thickness of a finger ; a few days

later it was like a child's arm. As the present time it yields no less than 122,000 litres [1] per day.

They saw the spring, and Bernadette into the bargain. The distrust and disappointment of the day before were quite gone ; they greeted her with the exclamation, ' Here comes the saint ! ' It was in vain, however, that Bernadette knelt down that day ; the lady did not appear to her.

And yet the joy over the fountain and the admiration for Bernadette were both justified. A fount of healing, a health-giving water, had really sprung up here— although differing in nature from the sulphuric springs in the Pyrenean watering-places. For there was a witness to the nature of that healing fountain that Bernadette had found, in the Gospel which was that day read in all Catholic churches, and which said :

' After these things was a festival day of the Jews, and Jesus went up to Jerusalem. Now there is at Jerusalem a pond, called Probatica, which in Hebrew is named Bethsaida, having five porches. In these lay a great multitude of sick, of blind, of lame, of withered, waiting for the moving of the water. And an angel of the Lord descended at certain times into the pond ; and the water was moved. And he that went down first into the pond after the motion of the water was made whole of whatsoever infirmity he lay under.' [2]

---

[1] About 27,000 gallons. A gallon contains about 4½ litres.
[2] St. John v. 1–4. The Gospel on the Friday after the first Sunday in Lent. It happened that this Friday in 1858 was February 26.
In all instances throughout the book, where quotations from the Gospels occur, the Douai version has been used.—*Translator's Note.*

VI

THE ATTITUDE OF THE CLERGY

On Saturday morning, February 27, 1858, the parish priest of Lourdes, Monsieur l'Abbé Peyramale, was walking up and down in his garden, reading his breviary. A sound as of a gate being shut made him look up ; a young girl had come into the garden and was coming towards him. The priest stopped, his penetrating glance under the bushy eyebrows resting on the visitor who was timidly approaching him.

'Who are you ? What do you want ? ' he asked brusquely.

And Bernadette—who, by her own admission was ' more afraid of Monsieur le Curé than of the police '— mentioned her name.

'Oh, so it's you, is it ? ' exclaimed the Abbé Peyramale, and his face grew sterner even than before. ' There are some fine tales being told about you ! Come inside ! '

With her heart in her mouth, Bernadette followed the imposing figure of the priest.

'Well, then, what do you want ? ' the priest asked again, when they were in his study.

And Bernadette, who had come straight from Massabieille, where the lady had that morning appeared to her, answered :

'The lady in the grotto has told me to tell the priests that she wishes to have a chapel built at Massabieille, and that is why I have come.'

'The lady in the grotto—who is she?' asked the Abbé Peyramale, pretending to have heard nothing.

'She is a very beautiful lady, who shows herself to me at the grotto.'

'A lady belonging to Lourdes? Someone you know?'

'No, she does not belong to Lourdes. I don't know her.'

'And you undertake to bring messages of that kind for a person you don't know?'

'Oh, Father, this lady is not like any other lady!'

'What do you mean?'

'That she is so beautiful, so lovely—people must be like that in Heaven!'

The priest shrugged his shoulders.

'You have never asked the lady her name?'

'Yes, but she only looks down and smiles, and doesn't answer me.'

'She can't speak, then?'

'Yes, she speaks to me every day.'

'Tell me, anyhow, how you came to know her.'

Bernadette then told the priest all that had happened since the 11th of February. Meanwhile the Abbé observed her carefully, and it was evident to him that she invented nothing, but only told him what she believed she had seen. When she had finished he said:

'And this lady has ordered you to tell the priests in Lourdes that she wishes a chapel built out there?'

'Yes, Father.'

'Would you have undertaken to bring a similar message for other ladies here in the town?'

'Oh, Father, there is a great difference between the lady I see and other ladies.'

'Yes, I should think so, indeed! A lady who won't tell you her name, who lives in a grotto and goes about barefoot in the middle of winter! No, my little girl, it's all imagination!'

The priest stood up. Bernadette remained seated, her head bent. After having walked up and down the room once or twice, Father Peyramale stopped in front of her.

'Tell the lady who has sent you that it is not the custom of the parish priest of Lourdes to have any dealings with people he does not know, and first of all she must tell me who she is. If she does not, she need not trouble to send me any more messages.'

Without answering a word Bernadette stood up, curtsied, and left. On Sunday, February 28, Monday, March 1, and Tuesday, March 2, she was at the grotto as usual, and the vision appeared to her on all of the three days. On the morning of March 2 she again stood before the Abbé Peyramale, this time accompanied by one of her aunts, Basile Castérot.

'Well,' said the priest, 'what did the lady say?'

'Oh, Father, she told me to repeat to you that she wants to have a chapel there, and she said besides, "I wish them to come here in a procession!"'

'Chapel! procession!' exclaimed the Abbé Peyramale, now losing patience. 'And what right has this lady to ask for chapels and processions? Now, my child, either you are telling a lie, or this lady is pretending to be the Blessed Virgin—for that is what she wants to make me believe she is. Besides, it is for the Bishop of Tarbes, not for me, to decide in matters of this kind—the lady really ought to be aware of that !

'But it is time there was an end of this. If, therefore, your lady is the person she is evidently pretending to be, she can easily give me proof of it. You say she appears in the grotto above a rose-bush ? Very well. Ask her from me to cause that rose-bush to put forth flowers one of these days ! When that happens I will believe you, and then I promise to go with you to Massabieille.'

The miracle asked for by Father Peyramale did not happen. But here and there in Lourdes people began to talk about all sorts of other miracles—about strange and wonderful things said to have been effected by *the water from the grotto.* Some workmen had put up a small wooden pipe which conveyed the water down to a little basin that they had dug out, and there were already sick persons who began to drink of the water and to step into the pool.

The first to be healed in this way was the stone-cutter, Louis Bourriette. It was a fact well known to every one in Lourdes that one of his eyes had been injured, nearly twenty years ago now, by a stone splint. In the course of time the other eye had also become weak, and it seemed probable that he would eventually become totally blind. As soon, therefore, as Bourriette heard about the spring at Massabieille, the hope of a cure dawned in him and he sent his daughter out for some of the water. It was still muddy, but Bourriette was not to be daunted. In fullest trust he bathed the injured eye and discovered, almost at once, that he could begin to see with it again. After each fresh application of the water his sight improved, and when, on the following day, he met Dr. Dozous, who had had him under treatment, he went up to him and said, 'I am cured!' 'It is impossible,' was the answer. 'The injury to your eye was organic.' As Bourriette persisted in his assertion, however, the doctor at last took out a note-book, wrote a few words in it, put one hand over the sound eye, and with the other held the writing before the injured one, certain that Bourriette, as usual, would be unable to read a single word. There was great consternation—for several passers-by had stopped to watch this consultation in the open street —when the patient read :

'Bourriette suffers from incurable amaurosis and he will never be better.'[1]

Bourriette's cure was a permanent one, and in a statement made on November 17, 1858, at the desire of the Bishop of Tarbes, Dr. Dozous declared : 'I have examined both of Bourriette's eyes and found them quite equal, both in shape and in the organisation of the individual parts. Both pupils re-acted normally when subjected to rays of light. In the right eye a scar was still visible, otherwise there was no trace of the injury that had once occurred to it.'

Other cures succeeded this first one. Sufferers who had spent long weeks or months on beds of pain, and who had been given up by physicians,

---

[1] Bourriette a une amaurose incurable, et il ne guérira jamais.— Cp. Dr. Dozous, *La Grotte de Lourdes, sa fontaine, ses guérisons*, and Dr. Boissarie, *Lourdes* (Paris, 1894), pp. 88–92.

declared that they had been cured by the water from the grotto. Jeanne Crassus, who had for ten years had a paralysed hand, dipped it in the spring, and the strength of the hand was restored to it. A child of two, Justin Bouhohorts, who was already dying, came back to life when his mother, with the courage of despair, plunged him into the icy cold water. Dr. Vergez, physician at the watering-place of Barèges, and Professor of Medicine at the University at Montpellier, declared of this last-mentioned cure : ' Never would any doctor have prescribed, for a child in an extreme state of exhaustion, in fact, almost dying, an icy cold bath lasting eight or ten minutes. In order to effect the cure of her child, Madame Bouhohorts has used means which are directly opposed to experience and reason. The cure, however, has not only been instantaneous, but the child who never before could walk is now able to stand on his feet. It is an instantaneous cure without any convalescence.'

A fortunate cold-water cure, it will be said. Perhaps a still more fortunate one was that by which the boy Henri Busquet was healed of a scrofulous sore on the neck after one night's treatment with a bandage dipped in Lourdes water.

Accounts of these and other marvels went all over the district, and when the last of the fifteen days dawned, on which Bernadette had promised to come to the grotto, from fifteen to twenty thousand people were assembled at Massabieille. It was the 4th of March, and eye-witnesses—such as Estrade and Dr. Dozous—relate how great the throng was, how they climbed up the rocks, into the trees, how even the river bank on the opposite side was densely packed. There were many who expected that the miracle asked for by the Abbé Peyramale would happen on that day, and that they would see the briar-rose flower before their very eyes. Bernadette arrived accompanied by two *gendarmes* who made way for her through the crowd. Her ecstasy took its usual course, but those who stood nearest to her saw that she was weeping, and thought it would be because the mysterious lady was bidding her good-bye. Nothing at all happened of all they had been expecting—no roses sprang forth from the bare thorns, and the lady did not make herself visible to them all.

When Bernadette came to herself again she was surrounded by a number of curious persons who asked what the lady had said at parting.

' She smiled to me as she disappeared, but she did not say good-bye.'

' Will you still come here, now that the fifteen days are over ? '

' All my life I will keep on coming here,' said Bernadette.

VII

THE FEAST OF THE ANNUNCIATION—' I AM THE IMMACULATE CONCEPTION '

BERNADETTE went regularly to school and instruction in the catechism and every day paid a visit to Massabieille. But it was not as before, that she felt irresistibly drawn to the spot ; she went there as she would go, for instance, to church, or to see a good friend. And so the days sped, quickly and monotonously ; the month of March was waning, the Feast of the Annunciation (March 25) was drawing near.

From time immemorial this feast has been celebrated with particular solemnity in the Pyrenees. The population of Lourdes generally chose this day for a pilgrimage to one of the numerous shrines of the Blessed Virgin ; in preference to Our Lady of Garaison or Our Lady of Béttharram. In the year 1858 the pilgrimage was made for the first time to the spot which was later to be known throughout the world as the shrine of Our Lady of Lourdes.

Bernadette, too, on that festal spring morning, felt drawn to the bare rock and the grotto with the rose-bush, which was now beginning to put forth leaves, though not yet flowers. Pious hands had arranged a little chapel within the grotto, with a statue of the Holy Virgin, and numerous tapers burned before it day and night.   Votive offerings were hung up there and no one left the place without laying a gift at Our Lady's feet. In the course of time quite a small treasury was accumulated there ; it was not guarded by any one, but no one would have dared to touch it.

Bernadette was drawn to Massabieille, not like the other pilgrims, but in the way she knew so well from the beginning, when the lady called her.   With her heart beating fast for very joy she threw her *capeline* over her head and hurried out by the path to the wood. A number of young girls and pious women were already assembled in prayer before the grotto—and oh, wonder ! the 'lady' was there too !   Already a long way off Bernadette saw the familiar light shining in the niche of the rock—the lady was there before her and stood smiling and waiting for her—like a mother for a child who has overslept herself.

'After I had knelt down before the lady,' Bernadette afterwards related, 'I first asked her pardon for having come so late.   She gave me to understand that it did not matter.   Then I told her how glad I was to be allowed to see her again, and after I had in this way unburdened myself to her, I took up my rosary. While I was praying the thought came to me that I would ask her now what her name was, and after a little time I could think of nothing else.   I was afraid that she might be vexed if I again asked a question which she had always refused to answer, and yet there was something that seemed to force me to speak.   At last I could not keep the words back any longer, and I asked the lady to be so kind as to tell me who she was.

'As she had done before, the lady bent her head and smiled but did not answer.   I don't know how it was, but I had more courage and I asked her again if she would not trust me with her name.

' Again she smiled and bent her head, but still she said nothing.'

' Then I folded my hands, and while I admitted that I was unworthy of so great a favour, I repeated my request the third time.'

' The lady was standing above the rose-bush and showed herself as on the wonder-working medal.[1] When I made my request the third time she looked grave and seemed to humble herself deeply before God. Then she lifted up her hands, laid them against each other on her breast, and looked up to Heaven. After that she slowly took them apart again, and as she bent forward towards me she said in a voice that trembled, ' I am the Immaculate Conception.'[2]

Bernadette always stopped at this point in her story, overcome by her feelings, as she reproduced the gestures and attitude of the heavenly apparition. When she had finished her account the first time in Estrade's house, she turned to Mademoiselle Estrade and asked—embarrassed at being so ignorant—' But, mademoiselle, what do those words mean—The Immaculate Conception ? ' And all the way to the house of the priest, to whom she could now at last tell the Lady's name, she went on repeating the words to herself, so that she might not forget them ; ' Immaculada Counceptiou, Immaculada Counceptiou ! '

---

[1] That is to say, with outstretched arms, and hands open and turned outwards, liké those on Thorwaldsen's statue of Christ. The wonder-working medal was struck in commemoration of an apparition of the Blessed Virgin to Catherine Labouré in a chapel in the Rue du Bac in Paris in November, 1830.

[2] In Bernadette's dialect : ' Qué soy ér Immaculada Counceptiou.'

VIII

THE DOGMA OF DECEMBER 8, 1854—THE APPARITION OF APRIL 7—THE AUTHORITIES INTERFERE

SEVERAL times the writer who is relating these events has had occasion to observe, that it is not only ignorant little girls in the Pyrenees, but also doctors of philosophy in Northern Europe, and journalists on the staff of big daily papers in the most enlightened capitals, who do not know the meaning of the expression, *conceptio immaculata*. As an instance : when the radical Swedish professor, Knut Wicksell (last year or the year before), was prosecuted for blasphemy, it was commonly said that he had spoken contemptuously about the ' immaculate conception.' It seemed to me, before I knew the details, that it was hardly likely there would be so much sensitiveness in Lutheran Sweden over a particularly Catholic dogma, and it did eventually appear that what Wicksell had attacked, and what the papers judged to be the 'Immaculate Conception' was—the Virgin Birth of Christ ! Moreover, grey-headed Protestant theologians have maintained to me, and in spite of my denial insisted on maintaining, that this opinion was right, and they have referred me to what they considered to be the doctrine of the Church, namely, that natural conception

E

was sinful and that the supernatural therefore was alone ' immaculate.'

With these experiences in mind, therefore, I do not consider it inopportune if I explain here that the Catholic dogma of the Immaculate Conception embodies a quite different idea. It states only this : That the Mother of Jesus, the Blessed Virgin, was, from the first moment of her existence, exempt from that stain of inherited, original sin, in which all other children of Adam and Eve come into the world. This doctrine is found already in the teachings of such Fathers of the Church as Irenæus and Ephraim ; the Franciscans contended for it all through the later Middle Ages ; Sixtus IV, in 1447, in Rome inaugurated the Feast in honour of Mary's Immaculate Conception ; and Clement XI promulgated it as a doctrine for the whole Church in 1708. It was, therefore, only the climax of a long development when Pius IX, by his Bull, *Ineffabilis Deus*, of December 8, 1854, solemnly confirmed the doctrine that Mary, from the first moment of her conception, for the sake of her Son and Redeemer, Jesus Christ, was preserved from every stain of original sin, and declared this dogma to be revealed by God and a clause in the Catholic Faith.[1]

On December 8, 1854, on the Feast of the Conception of Mary, Pius IX had defined the dogma of the Immaculate Conception.

[1] The following extract from the text of the Bull is taken from Deuzinger's *Enchiridion*, 10th edition, No. 1641 :
' . . . declaramus, pronuntiamus et definimus, doctrinam, quae tenet, beatissimam Virginem Mariam in primo instanti suae conceptionis fuisse singulari omnipotentis Dei gratia et privilegio, intuitu meritorum Christi Jesu Salvatoris humani generis, ab omni originalis culpae labe preservatam immunem, esse a Deo revelatam atque idcirco ab omnibus fidelibus firmiter constanterque credendam.'

On March 25, 1858, on the Feast of the Annunciation, the day when the Word became Flesh, as Mary bent her head and said to the Angel, ' Be it unto me according to Thy Word '—on that day she herself stood in resplendent glory before another of her sex who had found favour with God,—and answered, when asked her name, ' I *am* the Immaculate Conception.'

' The Mother of the Lord,' says Lasserre, ' did not say, " I am Mary Immaculate." She said, " I *am* the Immaculate Conception ! " as if to emphasise the essential character of the privilege which had been given to her alone since Adam and Eve were created by God. It was as though she had said, not " I am pure," but " I am purity itself "; not " I am a Virgin,' but " I am Virginity living and incarnate." It is not a quality in her, it is her very essence.

' Mary is more than conceived without sin, she is the Immaculate Conception itself, that is to say, the archetype of humanity itself without sin, of humanity as it came from the hands of God in the Garden of Eden. . . . .

' When you wish to obtain pure water from a muddy source, you take a filter and cleanse the water from its grossest impurities. After this you pass it through a second filter and then a third, and so on. Then a moment comes when the water is perfectly clear and sparkles in the glass like liquid diamonds. This is what God did when mankind became impure at the source. He chose out a family and watched it from century to century, from Seth to Noah, from Shem to David, from David to Joachim and Anne, the parents of the Blessed Virgin. And when the

E 2

human blood was thus purified, through fifty generations of patriarchs and just, there came into the
world a being without stain, a child of Adam without
his guilt. Her name was Mary, as Virgin she became
Mother—the Mother of Jesus Christ.'

That which had now happened at Massabieille
was nothing less than the direct supernatural confirma-
tion of the dogma which Pius IX had four years earlier
—to use the words of an indignant Swedish poet [1]—
' flung in the face of the civilised world.' Such an
event, on which attention was already concentrated
within large circles in the Catholic Church, could not
but cause uneasiness amongst those men who governed
France at that time, and whose ideal was a steady,
sensible religion, which should be a social power and
contain the least possible elements of the supernatural.
Already on March 10 the Prefect of the department of
the Hautes Pyrénées, Baron Massy at Tarbes, had
received a communication from the Minister of Church
and Education, M. Rouland, asking for information
about the occurrences at Lourdes. And on April 12
a fresh ministerial communication arrived, stating,
amongst other things, that it was important that there
should be an end to scenes which could ultimately only
imperil the best interests of the Church and weaken
the religious feelings of the population. Strictly
speaking, no one had any right to erect a chapel or other
public place of worship without the joint permission
of the civil and ecclesiastical authorities. It would
therefore be desirable to take immediate steps for the
closing of the grotto which has been transformed into
a sort of chapel.

[1] Victor Rydberg.

'It is probable that practical difficulties will be attached to a sudden exercise of this right. It must therefore be sufficient to hinder the young girl in question from frequenting the grotto, and to take such measures as will, little by little, draw away the attention of the public from the spot, by gradually restricting the number of visitors.

'Moreover, Monsieur le Préfet, it is desirable that you should put yourself in communication with the clergy ; and I would suggest that you approach directly the Bishop of Tarbes. I authorise you to say to his Lordship that I am not disposed to submit any longer to a state of things which will serve as a pretext for fresh attacks on the clergy and religion.'

It was now the Prefect himself who had to accomplish that in which neither M. Dutour nor M. Jacomet had succeeded. The latter had even seen his orders disregarded by the Soubirous, and in the accomplishment of his task the Prefect had to seek help from the ecclesiastical authorities.

In the meantime Bernadette faithfully continued her visits to the grotto. The water rushed merrily through its wooden conduit down to the basin and increased in volume from day to day. And on the Wednesday of Easter Week, April 7, the Blessed Virgin appeared once again to the little seer. Estrade was not present on this occasion, but Dr. Dozous gives the following account :

'Bernadette, as usual, held her rosary in her left hand and a lighted candle in her right. . . . Suddenly it happened that as she wished to join her hands together she held the candle under her left hand, which was so spread out that the flame found a way out between the fingers. Contrary to all reason and experience the flame did not seem to affect the hand in any way whatever.

'Astonished at this, I prevented others from interfering, took out my watch and observed the phenomenon for a whole quarter of an hour. At last Bernadette again separated her hands.

'When the ecstasy was over she arose and prepared to leave. I stopped her and asked her to show me her left hand. I did not find the least trace of burning anywhere.

'I then had the candle re-lit and held it under Bernadette's left hand.

'"You are burning me!" she exclaimed, and quickly withdrew her hand.

'Many others besides myself observed this incident. I mention it just as it occurred without offering any explanation.'

The remarkable, nay the inexplicable, element in the incident narrated by Dr. Dozous is not Bernadette's insensibility. This has also been noticed in nerve patients. The peculiarity in Bernadette's case consists in the fact that the hand is not affected by contact with the flame. Even the most complete catalepsy cannot prevent the tissues from being affected in a natural manner by fire.

This event occurred, as stated above, on April 7. About a week later the Prefect, Monsieur Massy, called on the Bishop of Tarbes, Monseigneur Laurence, to convey to him the ministerial threat. The Bishop, however, was not in the least inclined to take any steps whatever in the matter, and preferred to await the course of events. The Prefect was therefore compelled to take action alone, and in the beginning of May he had the grotto cleared of the objects of devotion collected there. The road to it was closed, and all access to Massabieille and the surrounding land was forbidden. At the same time the Government had a sample of the water analysed, in order to determine whether it possessed any medicinal qualities. The analysis showed that the spring contained several minerals, especially lime, magnesia, oxides of iron and carbonate of sulphur. A later and more accurate analysis, made by a chemist in Toulouse, showed that a kilogramme of the water contained 8 centigrammes carbonic acid, 5 centigrammes oxygen, 17 centigrammes azote, traces of ammonia, 96 milligrammes carbonate of lime, 12 milligrammes carbonate of magnesia, traces of iron and carbonates of sodium, 8 milligrammes salt, traces of chloride of sodium, 18 milligrammes silicates, traces of sulphuric sodium, and traces of iodine.

The chemist who made this analysis, which is dated August 7, 1858, states that ' the water from the grotto of Lourdes may be considered as drinkable water of the same kind as that which is frequently found in mountainous districts with a chalky soil. The sample taken does not contain any substance which would contribute to the therapeutic qualities of the water : it can be drunk without any ill effects.' [1]

This excluded the hope of explaining from natural causes the cures which had been effected from the use of the water at Lourdes. As, however, the water was at the same time declared to be innocuous, it would seem

[1] This analysis can be found in Estrade's *Les Apparitions de Lourdes*, p. 251.

that permission might be given for the free use of it. Nevertheless, access to it was prohibited and several women who had defied the authorities were arrested and summoned before the higher court at Pau, but they were dismissed after having being kept two or three days in remand. The prohibition was not cancelled until October 5, at the direct intervention of Napoleon III, to whom the inhabitants of Lourdes had sent in a complaint, seizing the opportunity for this during the Emperor's visit to Biarritz. Free access to the grotto was granted, and, moreover, a few weeks later the *Moniteur Officiel* was able to announce that the Baron Massy had been promoted to the Prefecture of Grenoble, and the Commissary of Police, M. Jacomet, had received a better appointment at Avignon.

But before this day of victory dawned, the Blessed Virgin appeared yet once more to Bernadette, and bade her good-bye. During the time that the path to the grotto was closed, the little seer generally went out to a meadow on the other side of the Gave, from which she could look across the river to Massabieille. It was here that she had come on July 16, on the Feast of Our Lady of Carmel. Several women were gathered about her, and to their surprise and delight they saw that Bernadette's face began to shine once more in ecstasy. And Bernadette, beside herself with joy, pointed to the other side of the river in the direction of the grotto, where the briar-rose was now in full bloom, and cried: 'There she is! there she is! She is smiling to us across the barrier.'

Bernadette then appeared to hold a long conversation with her who was invisible to all the others.

It was late in the afternoon. The sun was sinking lower and lower. When it disappeared it was as if the light faded from Bernadette's face too. She had beheld the glorious vision for the last time.

She remained in Lourdes eight years yet. In November, 1858, the Bishop of Tarbes appointed a Committee before which Bernadette had to appear ; at the same time inquiries were made into the genuineness of the miraculous cures said to have taken place. The Committee worked for three years and a half, and on the basis of its inquiries Monseigneur Laurence, in a decree issued on January 18, 1862, at last made the pronouncement that the Blessed Virgin might be believed to have revealed herself at Lourdes. The devotion to Our Lady of Lourdes was permitted throughout the whole of the district, and the Bishop asked the Catholics of France to assist in building the church which the Blessed Virgin desired to be erected at the grotto. With this object in view he had already bought the whole of Massabieille, the island Le Châlet, and the land beyond Savy's Canal, south of the grotto in the direction of Lourdes.

Two years later a statue, the work of the sculptor Fabisch, from details furnished by Bernadette, was placed in the niche of the rock where the Blessed Virgin had revealed herself. It represents her at the moment when she uttered the words, ' I am the Immaculate Conception,' and Fabisch, when writing home, said, ' I have never seen anything so beautiful as Bernadette when I asked her to show me how the Blessed Virgin had looked when she said those words. Bernadette stood up, folded her hands and looked up to heaven. But neither Fra Angelico nor Perugino,

nor Raphael has ever painted anything so gentle
and yet so profound as the look in the eyes of this
simple, naïve young girl.'

And this was not a fortunate chance, something
that only happened once, and not oftener.

In another letter, of later date, the artist writes,
' No, as long as I live, I shall never forget this adorable
expression ! I have seen the works of the great
masters in Italy, but in none of them have I found
rapture and heavenly joy so adequately expressed.
And every time I asked Bernadette to sit to me, it
was always the same radiant glory that transfigured
her face.'

Fabisch was a talented artist, but not a Fra Angelico.
When, therefore, Bernadette saw the statue completed
she exclaimed, with unmistakable disappointment :
' Yes, it is beautiful, but it is not like her ! ' The
picture that was always present to her soul was so
immeasurably more glorious, and she tried again
and again to describe it to the artist.

On April 4, 1864, Fabisch's work was placed in the
niche with much solemnity. In the course of time
the stately basilica began to rise, on the top of the rock
of Massabieille, above the grotto. The first pilgrimage
came to Lourdes on July 25, 1864, the first of those
processions which the Blessed Virgin had expressed a
desire to see at the grotto, in her apparition on March
2, 1858. The little town of Loubajac, in the same
diocese as Lourdes, inaugurated the long train of
pilgrimages that were to find their way to Bernadette's
grotto as time went on, and that brought nearly four
million pilgrims to Lourdes during the years from
1867 to 1903.

THE BASILICA AT LOURDES

The basilica was completed in 1876 and was consecrated in the presence of thirty-five bishops, a cardinal, three thousand priests and one hundred thousand of the faithful. In order to give the constantly increasing number of pilgrims the opportunity of hearing Mass and receiving the Sacraments, it became necessary to build a second church in front of and below the basilica, at the foot of the Espélugues hill. This, the Church of the Rosary, was consecrated in 1901. And everything else in Lourdes has grown in proportion.

Bernadette did not witness this development. She had fulfilled her mission, testified to her vision; there was nothing more for her to do. On July 29, 1866, she took the veil in the Convent of Saint Gildard at Nevers, and entered the community of the same sisters whose school she had once attended. Bernadette Soubirous became Sister Mary Bernard.

Her convent life was not to last more than twelve years. In her extreme humility she always strove to avoid everything that could bring into remembrance the part she had played at Lourdes, and nothing was more painful to her than to be sent down to the parlour by her superiors, in order to satisfy the more or less pious curiosity of some casual visitor. 'The wild beast has to be shown,' she used to remark on such occasions. Even the celebrated Dupanloup, Bishop of Orleans, had some difficulty in obtaining an interview. He came to Nevers in a state of doubt, but, after a conversation of two hours with Bernadette, he declared: 'I have gazed into an innocent soul, and I have felt the irresistible power of truth.' Some months later the great opponent of Papal Infallibility went as a pilgrim to Lourdes.

It was only to children that Bernadette spoke willingly of her memories.

'Sister Mary Bernard,' a little girl asked her, 'is it true that you have seen the Blessed Virgin ? '

' Quite true.'

' Was she very beautiful ? '

' So beautiful,' Bernadette answered, in a voice that was husky with emotion, 'that I am only longing to die so that I may see her again ! '

She never deigned to look at the statues of Our Lady of Lourdes in the convent. If she could not avoid letting her eyes rest on one of these gaudy manufactured objects it was with a sigh, ' How hideous it is ! '

When the basilica above the grotto was about to be consecrated she was asked if she did not wish to be present ; her superiors were willing to give her permission to make the journey.

' No, thank you,' she said, with a sigh ; ' but I wish I could have gone there like a little bird ! '

She wished to see without being seen, noticed, and made much of. And, indeed, she never returned to the places which had been so dear to her, and where she had spent the happiest hours of her life.

In the convent Bernadette's duties were partly those of a nurse and partly of a sacristan. Meanwhile her health was failing. Her asthma had not left her, several times she coughed up blood, and on the whole her health was delicate. At last she spent most of her time in bed. When able to do so she did needlework, embroidering altar-cloths or the like, or she used her beloved rosary—or suffered. ' I am in pain,' she said to the sister who nursed her, ' but I am content. Besides, suffering is good for Heaven. What God wills, as He wills, and as much as He wills.'

In December 1878 she became seriously ill. During this illness she received two visitors, sent by the Bishops of Tarbes and Nevers, and to them she repeated once more all that she had so often before told about her visions. Face to face with death, and the Judge in Whom she believed, she solemnly declared : ' I have beheld the Blessed Virgin, I have seen her.'

Her illness, so rich in suffering, lasted all the winter and well into the spring. Yet once more Bernadette could live in spirit through all those most wonderful days in her life—from that 11th February, twenty-one years before, when she heard on the banks of the Gave, the same ' still, small voice ' in which of old, God revealed Himself to the Prophet, to that bright, sunny day, on the Feast of the Annunciation, when the Lady from Heaven had told her her glorious name.

Sister Mary Bernard died on the Wednesday after Easter, April 16, 1879, at three o'clock in the afternoon, with the crucifix in her hands, and with those words on her lips which she had so often repeated all through her life : ' Holy Mary, Mother of God. . . .'

IX

THE greatest difficulty that confronts the stranger who visits modern Lourdes for the first time would seem to be that of finding the grotto. On reaching the outskirts of the town, and after crossing one of the two bridges over the Gave, one enters into a series of gardens, bewildering in their number and extent. Avenues, lawns, flower-beds, gravel-paths, statues ; on the right and the left buildings that look like offices ; finally an immense, wide esplanade terminated by the low and broad façade of a church built in the Romanesque style, with a snow-white Madonna on a golden background above its wide open door. This esplanade is framed on both sides by semicircular, very slightly rising ascents supported on enormous stone-built arches, the ascents leading up to a second church, which up above raises its slender Gothic spire to heaven. The lower, Romanesque church is known as the Church of the Rosary, and is built like a great hall or rotunda, with room for thousands and thousands of pilgrims. The church above is the original basilica and consists in an upper church and a crypt hewn out of the rock of Massabieille itself. Underneath the steps up to the main doorway of the basilica a door opens on to a long, low corridor with marble walls, like the entrance to a Roman catacomb. This leads to the crypt.

The whole of the former island of Le Châlet, and the summit, as well as the eastern slope of the Espélugues hill, is covered with these gardens and hidden by these buildings. In order to reach the grotto you turn to the right through one of the arches on the north side of the Place du Rosaire. This brings you to a narrow strip of land situated between the hill and the river Gave. Here, too, the ground has been levelled and gravel paths have been made, and on the side nearest the water a stone parapet serves as a back-rest for a long bench, on which hundreds of persons can find seats. This bench and the river behind it is on the right; on the left, beneath the hill, there is first a small book-shop, then the *piscinæ* or bath-houses, three low buildings, in which the baths for invalids are situated, and which have taken the place of the primitive basin in which the water from the spring was first collected. Beyond the bath-houses one comes to a long row of taps, twelve in number, from which water is drawn, and then at last one arrives at the grotto, in front of which there is a large paved space, fenced in and provided with seats. One of the flag-stones is inscribed with the words : ' Place où priait Bernadette, 11 février, 1858.' On this spot Bernadette prayed on February 11, 1858.

The spring found by her has for a long time not been visible. It issues on the left side of the grotto, in the place where there is now a large metal slab or hatch, fastened with a padlock. From here the water is conducted through a concealed pipe, first to a tank above the twelve taps, from which everyone may drink of it, and then further down to the *piscinæ*, where it is used in the baths for the sick. There is one bath-room with three baths for the men and two rooms with six baths for the women. Each bath holds about 400 litres.[1] In the wall above the bath there are two taps, of which one is always running, so that the water is constantly being renewed. The baths are placed in a recess, with room on each side for those who have to lower the patient into the water. There is a curtain in front of each of these small bath cells ; in the space in front there are chairs and pegs for clothes. All the work connected with the baths is carried out free by a voluntary band of helpers—*les Hospitaliers de Notre Dame de Lourdes*—while the baths, too, are entirely free, and nothing is paid for residence in the hospital. Baths are given daily from nine to eleven and from two to four. Between eleven and two o'clock the baths are emptied and cleaned.

Even with a supply of over 120,000 litres [2] per day the water would not, however, suffice for the larger stream of pilgrims in the summer—often four or five hundred baths in one day. For this reason the clergy, to whom the Bishop of Tarbes has entrusted the administration of the church of the pilgrims and everything connected with it, collect the water from the spring during the night and in the winter, in a large reservoir which has been constructed underneath the Rosary Church. It was this precaution that some years ago gave rise to a sensational article in American and European papers, alleging that the water in the *piscinæ* did not come from the spring

[1] About 88 gallons.   [2] About 26,000 gallons.

at all, but was simply river water which the crafty priests had led into the baths.

On this rainy afternoon, then, after I have washed and had a meal at the hotel, I go across the Place in front of the Rosary and under the arches towards the *piscinæ*. It is just at the time when the bathing is going on, between two and four o'clock. A company of Belgian pilgrims, about twelve hundred persons, have arrived in the morning and have now brought their sick, about two hundred, to the baths. In front of the bath-houses there is a large enclosed space which is reserved for the patients, nurses, and the *brancardiers*, the other voluntary corps of helpers at Lourdes. Its members can easily be distinguished by the leather straps over their shoulders, which they use when they carry patients on their stretchers. Some of these assistants, as well as the *hospitaliers*, are resident in Lourdes, but each train of pilgrims also brings its volunteer helpers, who complete the *personnel* of the organisation. The *brancardiers* undertake the work of conveying the patients from the hospital and back, either on stretchers or in small, light ambulance carriages.

Just as I arrive the enclosure is full of these ambulances, waiting in front of the *piscinæ*. Most of them are empty—the patients are sitting on benches at the entrance to the baths and awaiting their turn. Hospital nurses, doctors, and the leaders of the pilgrimage, easily recognised by their badges in the Belgian colours, are going about amongst them. The other pilgrims, too, wear ribbon badges, but smaller ones, and a number corresponding to their number in the pilgrim register, which makes it possible, in the event

F

of a cure, to identify them at once and find the papers relating to their case.

Owing to the rain I do not see much of the patients themselves—umbrellas are put up over them, or they lie on their stretchers covered with tarpaulins and other protections from the rain. I have stopped to see the men's section, and everything is done very quietly—only now and then there is more movement, when the door to the baths is opened and a couple of patients come out after their bath and new ones are admitted. One is reminded of the consulting-room of some great doctor—only the waiting-room is in the open air. I notice a man who is sitting quite close to the door, and who will evidently go in next— his face is violet—of a strange, dead metallic hue— as if he was saturated right to the skin by some horrible poison. His reddish, inflamed eyes are lowered ; between his fingers, also violet, the rosary beads are gliding. . . .

For all pray here who possibly can. The space outside the enclosure is thronged with people, not inquisitive spectators, but relatives, friends, acquaintances, compatriots of the patients—all pilgrims who, under the glistening umbrellas, in hushed voices murmur the prayers of the rosary. And in the space within the enclosure a tall young priest now steps forward, uncovers his head in the pouring rain, and in a loud voice begins a series of prayers sounding strangely impressive in the strong Flemish language, and repeated in chorus by all those standing about me. They are short invocations, cries to God for help, impetrations, hurled up towards the grey, apparently indifferent and relentless, heavens.

'Heiligste hart van Jesus, genees onze zieken,' prays the Flemish priest, and round about me all murmur the same prayer, 'Most Sacred Heart of Jesus, heal our sick!'

'Heiligste hart van Jesus, bekeer onze zondaars,' he continues, and all say after him, 'Most Sacred Heart of Jesus, convert our sinners.'

'Heiligste hart van Jesus, ontferm u onzer,' 'Most Sacred Heart of Jesus, have mercy on us.'

For a moment he pauses. The rain is streaming down his black hair, his lofty brow, over his strong and beautifully modelled features. His deep-set eyes are particularly wonderful—their earnest, powerful, enthusiastic expression—as in one whose faith can move mountains. . . .

Again he raises his voice; now he is calling on Mary :

'Onze lieve vrouw van Lourdes, onbevlekte maagd, Moeder van God, genees die zieken voor de bekeering der zondaars!' 'Our dear Lady of Lourdes, immaculate Virgin, Mother of God, heal the sick that sinners may be converted!'

'Onze lieve vrouw van Lourdes, genees onze zieken!' 'Our dear Lady of Lourdes, heal our sick!'

'Onze lieve vrouw van Lourdes, bekeer onze zondaars!' 'Our dear Lady of Lourdes, convert our sinners.'

'Onze lieve vrouw van Lourdes, bid voor ons.' 'Our dear Lady of Lourdes, pray for us.'

Again a pause, then the young priest takes out his rosary and I pass on, while the salutations to Mary begin to resound behind me. A few minutes' walk and I stand before the grotto.

I had imagined it larger. The pictures of it give one the impression that it is rather large. I wonder still more at finding that the marble statue in the niche above the briar-rose is so small.

At this moment the space in front of the grotto, fenced in with chains, is quite full of stretchers and invalid chairs, patients being carried or wheeled along after their bath. A couple of children are placed in the front row—underneath the umbrellas I see two little, leaden-hued faces, and small white, frail fingers fumbling with a rosary—and such wistful, such pleading eyes, fastened on the white statue, on her who has helped so many others, and who could help them too. . . . They are boys—one of them has continual fits and throws off all rugs and coverings ; his father, who looks like a working man, and who is kneeling in prayer behind the stretcher, patiently puts everything right again each time. . . . Another child is continually thrusting his head forward, his eyes are closed, a little froth is oozing from the half-open lips— a *brancardier* eases the pillow under his head.

I stand a few moments looking out over the stretchers. The rain is ceasing and umbrellas are being closed. The patients in the first row are all children, small, poorly-dressed boys—they are fully dressed so that one sees their rough, common clothes —and with such wasted, tortured, earth-coloured or ashen faces. There is no sight so heart-rending as that of suffering children—cheeks that ought to be plump and rosy, and instead are pale and sunken ; eyes that ought to glow with the joy of life, and sparkle with merriment, are instead dull, listless, almost lifeless. . . .

THE GROTTO

I go on, into the grotto; I cannot bear the sight
of the sick children. . . . There is an iron railing
before the grotto—with *Entrée* on one side and *Sortie*
on the other. Up above there are rows of crutches,
left there by those who have been cured . . . there are
many more on the wall of the rock outside. Immediately below the statue there is a large iron stand,
full of burning candles of all heights and sizes, from
the large ornamented ones as thick as a boat's mast
and costing a hundred francs, to the small, thin ones
no bigger than a 'farthing dip' and costing fifty
centimes. Behind this first large stand there is
another, a little lower. And the whole of the innermost part of the grotto, where the rock slopes low
down, is laid out like one solid bed of flames, with
row upon row of iron spikes on which the candles are
impaled. There is just room to walk between the
altar in the middle of the grotto and this garden of
flames. An old man with a motionless face, the
colour of brown parchment, and with a coarse, blue
apron over his clothes, goes about unceasingly and
trims the candles, cleans the sockets or spikes by
scraping off the wax that has dripped, and changes
them as they burn down and can be moved in where
the roof is lower, lights new candles and puts them
in the place of those that have gone out, receives the
candles one wishes to put up and puts them in a box
where hundreds of others are already waiting, and
from which he is continually renewing his supply.

It is warm here under the sooty, lowering roof,
warm and extraordinarily quiet. Many people are
continually passing through; they touch with their
fingers or lips that place in the rock which is just

below the Madonna niche, and on going out place an offering in the large copper vase. Many stay a little while, kneeling on the *prie-dieus* ranged on the left underneath the rock, or on the paved floor of the grotto. . . . Yet notwithstanding those who pass out and those who stay, the stillness is as deep as if one were far away amongst lonely mountains. . . . The old watchman moves noiselessly to and fro amongst his candles; one hears only the faint guttering of the flames, the metallic ring of coins dropping into the bronze urn, and the sighs breathed forth by those at prayer about one and behind one. . . . the sighs that here, on this consecrated spot, the goal of such ardent longings and such long journeys, rise from a burdened heart, and trembling between doubt and confidence rise to the Blessed among women: 'Our dear Lady of Lourdes, immaculate maid, Mother of God, heal our sick, that sinners may be converted.'

X

BENEDICTION IN FRONT OF LE ROSAIRE—
THE UNQUENCHABLE FIRE

IT is four o'clock—the *piscinæ* are being closed.

On the space in front of them and before the grotto the long train of Belgian pilgrims moves away— carried, wheeled, led by the arm—crippled, lame, blind, diseased and leprous—a crowd as piteous to behold as that which in far-off days, along the roads of Galilee and in the towns about the Lake of Gennesaret, thronged about the Master from Nazareth, and tried if they could but touch the edge of His mantle or the hem of His garment.

Slowly the sad procession moves in the direction of the hospital, home to ' Our Lady of the Seven Sorrows,' as the hospital in Lourdes has fittingly been called. But first a pause is made on the big ' Place,' that spreads out before the Rosaire in a sweeping curve, between the two ascents. Here is seen one of the most impressive sights to be witnessed in Lourdes, or indeed anywhere in the world, a sight that has not been equalled since the time of the Gospels, when Our Lord walked on this earth, and, as one of His apostles has said, ' went about doing good.'

On each side of the immense circular space the patients are ranged in their invalid chairs or on their stretchers. Behind them stand the *brancardiers* or stretcher bearers, the nurses, the relatives or friends of the sick who have accompanied them. In a wide circle outside, all the rest of us. Alone, in the middle of the great Place, a priest or two, to lead the prayers.

And now, from the porch of the Rosaire, and followed by priests in vestments, and acolytes with censers and lighted candles, steps forth an ecclesiastic in shining cope, with the Blessed Sacrament of the Altar, the Sacred Host, borne in a glittering monstrance. A canopy protects the Most Blessed Sacrament. Slowly the solemn procession approaches, comes down the steps along the *perron* of the church and moves towards the invalids. Opposite every single stretcher and every little carriage the procession stops, and while all around fall on their knees, the officiating priest blesses the sick with the uplifted monstrance. The Saviour Himself comes in the White Robe of the Host to each of these cripples and suffering ones who are lying in His path, as of old they lay along the dusty, sun-scorched roads of Galilee and Judæa. And, as at the marriage feast at Cana, it is His Mother who brings them to Him and pleads their cause with His Heart. Listen, it is said now as it was once outside the gates of Jericho or Capernaum : ' Jesus, Son of David, have mercy on us ! ' The priest, from the midst of the Place, with a ringing voice hurls forth these invocations, and in united chorus the assembled thousands echo his prayers and his cries.

' Lord, we adore Thee ! ' he exclaims, and round the Place the echo rolls like a wave,

' Lord, we adore ̦Thee ! '

' Lord, we hope in Thee ! ' And we all answer and repeat, ' Lord, we hope in Thee ! '

' Lord, we love Thee ! '

Yes, yes, we love Thee, as well as we can, imperfectly, weakly, selfishly ! We have so little compassion for others, so much for ourselves ! And yet it is not quite false when we say that we love Thee, Thou the purest, best, noblest of the children of men ! We do at least desire to love Thee, and would fain grow in love of Thee and learn to do Thy Holy Will.

' Hosannah, Hosannah, thou Son of David ! Blessed is He that cometh in the name of the Lord ! '

It is the cry of Palm Sunday, of the victorious entry into Jerusalem. It is echoed here, now, like a cry for help from the archways at the pool of Bethesda. . . .

' Thou art the Christ, the Son of the living God ! ' :

' Thou art my Lord and my God ! ' :

' Thou art the Resurrection, and the Life ! '

The voices rise in response—yes, resurrection and life is what all these dying ones, these corpses almost, are waiting for, hoping for.

' Thou art the Resurrection, and the Life ! '

' Save us, Lord, we perish ! ' cries the priest, like the disciples on that terrible night of the storm on the Lake of Gennesaret, and as though we all expected to see Him come walking upon the waters we pray in an agony of fear : ' Lord, save us, we perish ! '

' Lord, if Thou wilt, Thou canst make me whole. Lord, say but a word, and I shall be healed.'

Yes, Lord, if Thou wilt. . . Thou didst awaken the daughter of Jairus and the widow's son at Nain. Thou saidst to the centurion, ' Thy son liveth,' and the fever left him in that same hour.

' Jesus, son of David, have mercy on us ! ' :

' Jesus, son of Mary, have mercy on us ! ' :
' Mary, Mother of Jesus, pray for us ! '

One by one the loud invocations roll over the heads of the sick ; they respond in low murmurings, quiet and bent, fingering their rosaries. And slowly, solemnly the procession with the Sacred Host moves from one litter to another.

It was a priest from Montauban, the Abbé Lagardère, who, in 1888 conceived the idea of this Benediction of the sick in the open air, and since then it takes place daily at Lourdes, during the whole season of the pilgrimages. It is the close of the day for the invalids, as the Mass in the morning is the beginning, and often it has happened, just as the monstrance with God's White Heart (the expression is Robert Hugh Benson's) is uplifted in benediction over a sufferer, that one who has been declared incurable, given up by all physicians, has heard within him an all-conquering Talitha cumi, a mighty Ephphatha, a supernatural ' Arise, take up thy bed and walk ! '

I stand amongst the pilgrims in the large circle and see the Benediction given to one after the other of the sick. Wherever the canopy and the gold-glittering vestments of the priests and the incense and candles approach, they cause a breach in the human wall of those who fall on their knees. A moment after they rise, while the monstrance passes on like a flashing sickle, mowing down swath by swath. Slowly it comes to the place where I am standing—the procession is now only a couple of stretchers away—now it is next to us— now right in front of us. We all drop on our knees, our heads bent deep, and caring nought for the pools of water in which we kneel.

BENEDICTION OF THE SICK

For it is still raining—streaming—pouring. The
sky seems to have reserved one of its greatest cloud
bursts for this moment. The invalids are covered
with tarpaulins, rubber capes, raised hoods on the
ambulances and stretchers. We others protect ourselves as best we can under our umbrellas, while we
stand so close together that the water trickling from
the umbrella of one runs down inside the coat collar of
another.

And yet everything is done with the same undis-
turbed calm as though we had above us the brightest
blue sky of a summer day. The priests do not walk
one single step quicker, though their gold embroidered
copes are streaming with rain. The priest who gives the
Benediction does not pass over any of the sick, hurries
nothing, does not shorten or rush anything. And out
in the middle of the Place, which has gradually become
a lake of yellow water, stands the young Flemish priest
whom I saw this morning at the baths. It is he who
leads the prayers ; with the rain streaming from his
hair, drenched to the skin, his strong face raised to the
pitiless sky, he cries unweariedly up to this apparent
indifference to us poor human worms, indifferent to
our weal and woe, flinging prayer after prayer like
flaming arrows up through this wilderness of driving
clouds.

' Lord, we worship Thee ' :

' Lord, we hope in Thee ' :

' Lord, we love Thee ! '

In vain does the rain come down, in vain do these
merciless elements rage, as though they wished to
drown in their streaming waters all the fair aspirations
of poor human hearts. Faith unquenchable burns

like a fire that cannot be extinguished, that does not die, but only burns up afresh in a still more unconquerable prayer.

' Lord, we worship Thee ! ' is the cry of these unhappy ones, sorrowful, bowed down to the earth, crushed by the weight of life, in whose misery not a ray of sunshine, not a gleam of heaven's blue can be seen. . . .

' Lord, we hope in Thee ! ' confesses this defeated, conquered host, helpless and wounded to death. . . .

' Lord, we love Thee ! ' is the cry of the dying, while the storm beats over their last couch, and it seems as though every spark of hope must be quenched under the pouring rain. Lord, we love thee in spite of all, in spite of everything ! We are in Thy hands, and we know that Thou art our Father, and that not a sparrow falls to the ground without Thy will. . . . Lord, we love Thee ; Lord we love Thee !

THE RIVER GAVE

XI

A RECOVERY?—BUREAU DES CONSTATATIONS MÉDICALES—TWO RECOVERIES

BEING tired after my long journey and the new and strong impressions I have received, I go to bed early and wake up next morning at about seven o'clock. It is still cold, but the rain has ceased, the sun is shining, and the sky is a misty blue, with drooping clouds. I hear the rushing of the Gave beneath my windows, and a few birds singing in the hotel garden. All about the town and up behind the pilgrim church the mountains are ranged, large and green, with worn-looking places where the bare chalk shows.

I dress quickly, hurry over the bridge across the Gave and down through the gardens and across the esplanade to the grotto and the baths. The Belgian pilgrims are already there—and again I am stirred with emotion at the sight of these pale, leaden-coloured faces, and the everlasting repetition of the prayer, so pathetic in its very expression, ' Onze lieve vrouw van Lourdes, bid voor ons ! ' As on the previous day, I go into the innermost corner of the grotto, where the flames of the candles crackle in the deep silence, and where one is involuntarily overcome by one's feelings. Slowly and ceaselessly the scalding tears fill one's eyes, run down and burst forth again. It is as though the entire woe of the whole of mankind were concentrated in this place, and one can do nothing but weep and pray—saying the prayers of the rosary, that has been washed in tears and consecrated in blood—the rosary that has been called rich in sorrows, and that is to remind us of Him who prayed in the Garden of Olives ' and when He was sorrowful even unto death, He prayed the longer. And His sweat became as drops of blood trickling down upon the ground. . . .'

Presently, as I am about to leave, there is a sudden commotion in the crowd gathered in front of the grotto. A stretcher is quickly brought in and the bearers smile and wave their hands to everyone. ' Genesen, genesen ! ' passes in delighted tones from mouth to mouth, ' guéri, guéri ! ' Some one has been cured ! The crowd closes in, but the *brancardiers* take care that none of those outside come into the space before the grotto which is reserved for invalids. The stretcher is set down amongst the others, and round about me I hear in French and Flemish that the patient is a woman who has been paralysed and who can now move one hand after a bath at the wells.

I take careful note of myself at this moment. I realise that I am in a state of strange excitement. I have a feeling of being thoroughly shaken out of my usual folds. It seems as though I have been breathed upon by spirits from unknown worlds, and I am filled with fear rather than satisfaction. Here I am, suddenly confronted with something I cannot explain, which I have not the means to examine, nor the foreknowledge to judge. I am reminded of what was once said to me by a Danish Catholic, a devout and fervent old lady who had just come back

from Lourdes : ' They cried miracle ! miracle ! but,
really, *I* couldn't see any miracle ! '

And then I remember that there is a medical
institution at Lourdes, the so-called *Bureau des
Constatations Médicales*, and that I have a letter
of introduction to Dr. Boissarie, the physician who
has presided over this institution for many years.
On my way across the esplanade this morning I saw
the blue enamelled plate of the bureau somewhere
above a door, and directly after luncheon I direct
my steps to it, find the door, and notice that
the bureau is built underneath the ascent, between
two of the arcades supporting it. On one side of
the door there are two windows, provided with dull
glass panes ; one of them is furthermore protected
by iron bars. Above and between the windows
there is a statue of Saint Luke, the physician, and
the patron saint of the medical profession.

This bureau was established in 1882, under the
management of Dr. Boissarie's predecessor, de Saint
Maclou. Since then all pilgrims coming to Lourdes
in quest of health are required to bring with them
a medical certificate, as fully detailed as possible.
If they appear to have been cured, the bureau is
able, by means of this certificate, to form an opinion
about the patients, and, after an examination, to
determine whether any change has taken place in
their condition.

Dr. Boissarie, who has managed the bureau since
1883, is assisted in his daily work by Dr. Cox, an
Englishman. The bureau is, however, open to all
doctors—above all to those who accompany the
pilgrims, but next to them to all others. Thus, in

1892 it was visited by 120 doctors, in 1902 the number had risen to 268, in 1907 to 332, and in 1908 even to 625. During the last seventeen years the bureau has received altogether 4,117 doctors within its walls. And everything is open to these members of the medical profession, they can examine the patients for themselves, study the certificates, scrutinise the records of the bureau ; there is no secrecy, everything is done in the fullest publicity. Nay, not only the doctors, and not only a Zola (who was the guest of Dr. Boissarie in 1892, before he wrote his celebrated novel, ' Lourdes '), but every writer, every journalist, every educated person who is interested, has the same right to form an opinion based on the most complete personal observation.

I was aware of this, and yet it was with some trepidation that I approached this place where science sits in judgment on the miraculous. It was two o'clock, so that the bureau would be open. My knocking called forth a gruff *Entrez*—I opened the door and walked straight into the consulting-room, or whatever it ought to be called.

It is a large room, taking up the whole width of the ascent and with a door at the back opening on to the road along the river bank, behind the arcades. The walls and the vaulted ceiling are lined with light pitch pine. A couple of large frames, with a collection of photographs of those who have been cured, hang on one of the walls on the right as one steps in. There are benches covered in American leather against the walls,. a few chairs and bookshelves full of journals and documents. In the background one or two doors leading to the rooms where the patients are examined. And on the left, in front of the window overlooking the esplanade, there is a long, wide table, at which Dr. Boissarie himself is seated, with Dr. Cox at his side.

I deliver my letter of introduction to the senior doctor, who after rapidly glancing over it, hands it to Dr. Cox. Then he turns his clean-shaven, immovable lawyer face to me ; a couple of stern furrows run from the nose down about the tightly closed lips, and the pale blue eyes contemplate me keenly over the eye-glasses.

' Sit down there, so that we can see you.'

And I sit down in one of the leather-covered armchairs provided for patients and begin to give some information about myself. Then Dr. Cox joins in the conversation, and it turns out that he is a friend of Robert Hugh Benson, whose novel, ' The Lord of the World,' I have just begun to translate into Danish, and that he is also, like myself, an admirer of the Irish writer, another Catholic priest, Sheehan, the author of ' Luke Delmege,' ' My New Curate,' and many other impressive books.

But there is not much time to examine me, as we now hear the sound of many voices outside. Dr. Boissarie casts an alert glance to the right, towards the door. Dr. Cox puts my letter in a portfolio, and arranges his papers ; I rise from my chair, and before we know what is happening the room is full of people. No less than three patients, said to be cured, are brought in—one of them walks unaided, the second is on a stretcher ; the third, a middle-aged woman, sits upright on the arm of a stalwart attendant, carried like a child, and smiling and bowing to everybody.

G

In the train of the three patients follow Sisters of
Mercy, doctors, ecclesiastics, and inquisitive spectators.
More are threatening to come in, but a couple of
muscular *brancardiers* put their shoulders against
the door, get the key turned in the lock and the bolt
shot.   So now we are in peace and the examination
can begin.

Dr. Boissarie turns first to the patient on the
stretcher, a woman, like the other two, by the way.
She is not the patient whom I saw at the grotto this
morning—it is not a paralytic who has regained the
use of her hand, but a blind person who asserts that
she has received her sight.   The doctor asks for her
certificate, the number attached to her dress is
examined, and then Dr. Cox finds her certificate on
a large file.   Muttering to himself, Dr. Boissarie
runs through the paper and then turns to a young
Belgian doctor who is eagerly reading with him.

' And now she asserts that she can see ? '

A little nun, who is kneeling beside the stretcher
and supporting the patient's head, eagerly answers
that she does.

' What can she see then ? ' continues the old
doctor, with apparent sternness.   ' People, trees ? '

' She can see light,' explains the little nun.

' Will you open the eye,' Dr. Boissarie asks the
young Belgian.

He kneels down beside the stretcher, removes the
bandage and a tampon of cotton wool, and opens first
one and then the other of the patient's closed eyes.

Dr. Boissarie looks at them with interest, but
immediately shakes his head.

' Quite destroyed !   Impossible to see with those

eyes ! ' Involuntarily the good little nun's eyes become dimmed with tears.

' But, monsieur le docteur, she can really see light, she has said so herself ! '

The doctor, however, does not change his opinion, and our interest is centred on the next patient. It is she who was carried in before ; she is sitting now in one of the large armchairs in front of Dr. Boissarie, her face still beaming all over, while her papers are produced and given to Dr. Cox, who reads out their contents.

Her name is Marie Dillen ; she comes from Melsele, near Antwerp, is forty-five years old, a sempstress and unmarried. She has been delicate since the age of fifteen, and during the last ten years she has had frequent and sharp pains in the stomach and has often had to vomit her food directly after a meal. Taking nourishment caused her increasing difficulties ; at last she could hardly drink even milk. Since August of last year, that is 1908, she had been confined to bed. Her doctor diagnosed her case as an ulcerated stomach. Five times she had vomited blood.

' How much every time ? ' asks Dr. Boissarie, looking at the sempstress. But she does not understand French, and a Flemish priest who is present has to translate the question and act as interpreter for her. Picking at the fringe of her faded grey shawl she answers timidly, ' A great deal.'

' A great deal ! ' growls Dr. Boissarie. ' What does that mean ? Was it a basin full, a saucer, a soup-plateful ? '

' A soup-plate,' was the rather frightened answer. ' Quite black blood,' she adds.

G 2

' When did you arrive ? ' the old doctor asks.

' On Wednesday.'

' That was the 16th. And what was your journey like ? Did you eat anything on the way ? '

' No, nothing.'

' Nothing at all ? Nor drink anything either ? '

' No, nothing at all. I felt better when I didn't have anything.'

' And here, in Lourdes ? '

' I have had a little milk here.'

' And that makes you think that you are cured ? Do you feel better ? When did you begin to feel better ? '

The eyes of all present are on the poor Flemish sempstress, who is nearly out of her wits with embarrassment. She gathers all her courage together and says :

' I have had altogether four baths at the wells, the last was this afternoon. The other three did not do me much good, I was carried away on my mattress as miserable as I came. But to-day, when I was put into the water, I had an attack of most dreadful pain in my stomach—it went right through every part of my body, and then, directly after, it was all quite gone, I hadn't felt so well for years, and I felt that I was cured. . . .'

The doctor's face is inscrutable, not a muscle moves.

' Very well,' he says. ' If you are cured then you must be able to eat. Now go home, have your dinner, and come back to-morrow.'

The blind woman has already been taken away, now Marie Dilleri goes too. There remains the young girl who came on foot.

Her papers, too, are produced. Miss Julia
Witthamer, from Antwerp, twenty-seven years old.
She, too, suffers from an ulcerated stomach and has,
moreover, been twice operated, but the operations
have been unsuccessful : the pains and vomiting
have continued, and the young girl has been re-
duced to living on milk and tea. Like Marie Dillen,
she thinks that to-day, on the Feast of the Sacred
Heart, she has been cured by a bath—her third—
in the *piscinæ*. She is given the same advice as her
fellow-sufferer, to eat some food and come back on
the following day.

This finishes the programme for the day. Dr.
Boissarie rises and thus gives the signal for the
dispersal of the company. Soon after I am sitting
down to dinner at the hotel. A group of Belgians,
who have taken possession of the large table in the
middle of the room, are eagerly discussing the two
cures of the day.

XII

NEXT morning I am back at the bureau early and there I find, amongst doctors and priests, both Mademoiselle Witthamer and Marie Dillen.

The first named says that she had soup, an egg, bread and butter, as well as some wine last night, and that for her breakfast this morning she has had coffee and a ham sandwich, all of which would have been certain death for her not twenty-four hours before.

' Excellent, mademoiselle—just you go on like that,' says the old doctor. ' There is only one thing that is rather annoying, and that is, that my worthy colleagues at Antwerp have taken away so much of your stomach that there is not room enough in it any longer. You ought to have come here sooner, mademoiselle ! '

And turning to the rest of us the old doctor cannot repress an outburst of indignation at the mania of surgeons for operations.

It is now Marie Dillen's turn. Last night she ate an egg and two *croissants*, and drank a glass of wine—this morning she has drunk chocolate—all good things to which her stomach would previously have strongly objected. And triumphantly she presses her hand on this part, presses hard and long on that spot which was before so painful and where she feels nothing at all now. She is dismissed with the same advice as yesterday, and told to present herself for observation next day.

Julia Witthamer gets up to go too, and, with her, a fair and pale young girl who had been sitting beside her on the bench underneath the photographs of those who had been cured. A smile brightens up Dr. Boissarie's stern face and there is a look of paternal affection in his eyes when he sees the fair-haired girl. He gives her his left hand, ' la main du cœur,' and as he leads her to a chair beside the table he says, turning to us :

' This is Miss Augusta de Muynck, one of our visitors last year, who has come back now to show us that the cure has been maintained. . . . Oh, Cox, just look up Miss de Muynck's case—it is No. 10 in the register for 1908.'

The English doctor seeks out the papers in question and places them before his senior, who begins, in his slow, somewhat hesitating and yet firm manner, a little lecture in something like the following words :

Augusta de Muynck was born at Borgerhout, near Antwerp. Her father was a Catholic but not a practising one ; her mother was a very fervent Protestant, a Calvinist. None of the children, therefore, were baptized. When Augusta was six years old her father died. On his death-bed he sent for a priest, and the latter insisted on the children being baptized. Augusta was baptized at the same time that her father received Extreme Unction. When her mother heard of it she declared that she would have nothing more to do with

Augusta, and the child was therefore placed in the care of the Sisters of St. Vincent at Ecloo.   She stayed with them till her twenty-fourth year.

Augusta grew up in the convent in an atmosphere of piety.   At the age of twelve she made her first Communion, and at seventeen she began to go to daily Communion and has continued the practice for fifteen years now.   It was indeed fortunate for her that she had all the means of help that religion could give, to meet the trials that now awaited her.

For she had a sad physical inheritance to endure. Both her parents were consumptives and died of this disease ; as did also a sister.   And five years ago tuberculosis declared itself in a very serious form. On December 16, 1906, she underwent an operation at the hospital of St. Erasmus at Borgerhout.   This was followed by two other operations, the latter in Antwerp, on December 16, 1907, at the St. Camillus Hospital.   After these three operations her strength was quite exhausted.   She suffered unceasingly ; it was necessary to give her injections of morphia, and she could take no nourishment but a little milk, sometimes only water.

In this desperate condition she resolved to seek help at Lourdes.   She arrived here in May, 1908, practically in a dying state, after a railway journey of twenty-nine hours.   From Dr. de Preters, who had attended her in Antwerp, she brought the following certificate :

' Miss Augusta de Muynck is suffering from double peritonitis (*Pyo-salpinx*) of a tuberculous nature. The disease dates back to the begininng of 1906. She underwent a first operation on December 16, 1906 (removal of the left ovary and the Fallopian tube).

On May 11, 1907, laparotomy on the left side, opening of the abscess and draining. December 18, 1907, third laparatomy and draining of the abscess.'

Provided with this certificate, Miss de Muynck came to Lourdes on May 27, 1908. At this time she had a fistula in the abdomen, in which was inserted a rubber tube, $\frac{3}{8}$ of an inch in diameter, by means of which it was hoped to drain the abscess. During the journey, however, the tube was replaced by a gauze drain (*mèche de soie*) of the same size.

The suppuration is very copious, about half a litre[1] pus per diem. It seems as though the abscess were connected with the bladder ; a catheter is required to relieve the patient of water, and Dr. Moorkens, who accompanies the pilgrims, states that when he was called in to assist the patient on the journey, nothing but matter came from the instrument. The patient's nourishment consisted only of milk, water, and coffee. At Bordeaux she fainted and her condition seemed hopeless.

As stated before, she arrived here on May 27. On the 28th, a Thursday, she was carried on a stretcher to the *piscinæ* and given a bath. It had no effect, or rather, it seemed to make her worse. Nor did the Benediction of the Blessed Sacrament in the afternoon of the same day have the least influence.

On Friday, the 29th, she had two baths, one in the morning and one after mid-day. These baths caused an appreciable improvement. She was afterwards present at Benediction, and just as the Blessed Sacrament was carried back to the church, Augusta sat up on her stretcher and cried, ' I am cured ! ' At this moment

[1] A litre is equal to almost 2 pints.

all her linen was saturated with matter, the discharge had been so great. • She was placed on the stretcher again and brought back to the hospital, but there she sprang out of bed, changed her linen without assistance, and declared that she no longer felt any pain.

She had an excellent night. For the first time for many months, or rather years, she was able to sleep without morphia. Her appetite returned, and Augusta ate of everything that was offered her. On the next day, that is, the 30th, the rubber tube was removed as there was no longer any trace of suppuration, and the fistula closed up in the course of the day. In the evening Augusta dined at the adjacent hotel with an appetite that astonished every one present.

On the following day, May 31st, she again came to the bureau, and we ascertained that there was no longer any pain anywhere. The bladder had resumed its functions and contained no more pus.

It is over a year since then ; it is to-day June 19. Miss de Muynck has now returned in order to show us that her cure has been maintained. She brings a certificate from her doctor in Antwerp, stating that she had enjoyed good health from June 1908 to April this year. He does not deny that she is cured, but maintains that it is due to suggestion.

'For my part '—Dr. Boissarie sums up his little lecture—' it is clear to me that in this cure there is an almost instantaneous change for the better in an illness which, during three years, had ravaged all the organs of the pelvis. It is impossible, on the basis of medical science, to explain so rapid a re-absorption of an abscess which discharged half a litre of pus per diem. Besides, the bladder would probably be perforated and, in consequence of this, the surrounding organs would be affected.

' It is no less surprising that the patient's general health is all at once restored. We have here the case of a patient who has for three years been ravaged by fever, the secretion of pus, lack of nourishment, operations. She suffers from a tuberculous diathesis to which she would of necessity have succumbed—like her parents and her sister. Instead of this, she is now restored to health, and has since last year increased 18 kilogrammes in weight.[1]

' Perhaps it would have been possible to cure her elsewhere—at a sanatorium or the like—I do not know. In any case it would not have been with such suddenness, in a moment.

' Dr. de Preters says that Augusta is nervous. Even so, I do not believe that nervousness can have the least influence on a disease of a definitely tuberculous character. Even the most powerful suggestion can do nothing with an abscess of so serious a nature, and which has been allowed to continue so long. This explanation, therefore, does not suffice here, for in Augusta's case we are on purely tuberculous ground.'[2]

Dr. Boissarie ceases speaking and glances round at his audience. No one contradicts him. One of the foreign doctors bends towards Dr. Cox, whom I hear whispering the technical term *Pyo-salpinx* to him.

' To talk about nervousness or suggestion in this case is simply unreasonable,' concludes the old doctor. ' Augusta's cure is, from a scientific standpoint,

[1] About 36 lbs.   [2] (' En plein terrain tuberculeux.')

inexplicable.   Even if nature can repair such damage, she only does it slowly, in the course of years, little by little. . . . .'

Again he is silent for a few minutes.   His glance rests on the young lady who is sitting opposite him, and who has been quietly listening to his account of the disease as if it did not concern her.

'And now my child, show these gentlemen what the Blessed Virgin has delivered you from.'

Augusta de Muynck looks at the old doctor with her eyes full of tears.   Then she slowly takes out of her pocket a small parcel, unwraps it and shows us silently, almost solemnly, a small piece of india-rubber tubing. . . . .

XIII

AFTER having been present at the Benediction of the
sick on the Place du Rosaire, I am back in my room
again later in the afternoon. The morning after my
arrival at Lourdes I left the *hôtel de luxe* into which
I had been enticed at the recommendation of well-to-do
friends, and moved into a pension where I was just as
comfortable and in pleasant surroundings at a reasonable price. It is here that I have met the Belgians,
who seem to have made this pension their head-
quarters. From the window in my bright little
room I have the same view as from the hotel, at even
closer range. I look along the greenish-blue rushing
Gave towards the basilica, and have besides a glimpse
of the road between the river and the baths, and of the
square in front of the grotto. I have a small table
at the window and have now begun to read the book,
of which Dr. Boissarie has so kindly given me a copy—
the latest edition of his work, ' L'Œuvre de Lourdes,'
the continuation of his earlier great work, ' Les grandes
guérisons de Lourdes.'

At the bureau I had had an opportunity of speaking
a few words with Mademoiselle de Muynck. The
quiet, pale, and retiring young girl confirmed all that

I had heard from Dr. Boissarie, and yet I could not repress my doubts. Who knows, I ask myself, whether she was not improving in health when she set out for Lourdes ? The statement of Dr. de Preters was written a little while before her departure, perhaps the fistula had simply closed up on the way, and this process of healing was completed at Lourdes. Finally, it is possible that cold baths, such as those given at the *piscinæ*, may have a hitherto unknown effect on ulcers, peritonitis, and similar diseases.

But this last thought is so grotesque that I quickly dismiss it again. Besides, there are witnesses of the actual journey, that Augusta de Muynck's health was not improving on the way—quite the contrary. And yet, after all, it is difficult to rid oneself of doubts in the face of unusual events, and I look through Dr. Boissarie's book for other and more strongly certified cures.

Augusta de Muynck does not seem to be the only case of tuberculous peritonitis to be found in the records of Lourdes. I find several in Dr. Boissarie's book, and I select a case which seems to me to be particularly well attested.

' Marie Bailly's cure,' writes the doctor,[1] ' is one of the most interesting cases we have examined and authenticated. It is especially interesting from the standpoint of medical science ; it is impossible to find an examination more thoroughly and strictly conducted. For three years this young girl was under treatment in the hospitals at Lyons and Sainte Foy ; eight doctors attended her and gave evidence about her. One doctor 'of indisputable ability, and just as

[1] *L'Œuvre de Lourdes* (Paris, 1909. 1ome ed.), pp. 69–82.

unquestionable open-mindedness, accompanies her on her pilgrimage and never loses sight of her for a moment ; at Lourdes he goes with her to the hospital, to the grotto, to the *piscinæ*, everywhere.

' He watches her cure from hour to hour, from minute to minute ; he carefully notes the changes taking place before his eyes. It is, so to speak, a resurrection, of which he is given an opportunity of making a scientific record.

' *Marie Bailly's History.*

' Marie Bailly's father and mother both died of pulmonary tuberculosis. One of her brothers succumbed to the same disease, another is definitely tuberculous. It seemed that Marie Bailly, too, was to share their fate. " From my thirteenth year," she says herself, " our doctor at home, Dr. Terver, always advised me to live in the country and to avoid all mental work. I had a most distressing cough, frequently coughed up blood, and in winter suffered from an endless bronchitis. Finally, at the age of seventeen, in February 1896, I had an attack of double pleurisy. I was sent to St. Joseph's Hospital (at Lyons) to undergo an operation, but Dr. Chabalier refused to perform a puncture, as he thought I would not live through the night. I received the Last Sacraments and the Sister placed a medal of Our Lady about my neck.

' " Contrary to expectation I was better the next morning, and the doctors were of opinion that I would now be able to undergo an operation. They made two punctures and there was a discharge of about half a litre of fluid. I was confined to bed for five months. On leaving the hospital I had so far recovered that for the next two years I could live like other people.

' " Then my mother died in 1898 and I fell ill again. I had dropsy from head to foot, I could not breathe. Again I was sent to St. Joseph's, and put under the treatment of Dr. Clément. On my chart it was said that I suffered from nervous dyspnœa, and in the course of two months seven blisters were applied; sedative medicine was given, and also phosphorated lime and cacodylate.[1] None of it had any effect, and on April 17, 1899, I was transferred to the hospital at Sainte Foy."

' Marie Bailly was there placed in the care of Dr. le Roy, who treated her for pulmonary tuberculosis and laryngitis. He continued her treatment of arsenic in the form of pills and injections, gave her creosote, tried an air cure. The patient's voice became weaker, the disease seemed to reach the larynx, the vocal chords were painted with lactic acid. Dr. Fondet, who then examined the patient, prescribed a change of air, and in May, 1901, Marie Bailly went to Chabannes near Le Puy.

' Here the patient began to feel acute pains in the abdomen, and it seemed that the tuberculosis was about to extend its ravages in this direction. The summer passed badly, the general state of health became worse, the patient grew thinner and lost her appetite. The abdomen swelled up and became very tender to the touch. On November 7, 1901, the young girl came back to the hospital at Sainte Foy. Dr. le Roy now diagnosed the case as tuberculous peritonitis. The

---

[1] An arsenical preparation.

patient was confined to bed in the beginning of December and did not rise again until May 28, 1902, in Lourdes. In January, 1902, she had violent pains in the head, stiffness of the neck and other joints, feverish delirium. It was tuberculous meningitis, and the patient's condition was so low that one day Dr. le Roy was even prepared to sign the death certificate.

'Marie Bailly recovered from the meningitis, however, but the peritonitis pursued its course. In March Dr. le Roy sent his patient to St. Joseph's to undergo an operation—a last attempt to arrest the progress of the peritonitis.

'Marie Bailly was put under the care of Dr. Goullioud, surgeon at the hospital. He examined her and dictated his observations to one of the junior surgeons. The abdomen was swollen and tender, but did not contain fluid. He, too, diagnosed tuberculous peritonitis, but declined to operate as the patient seemed to him to be in far too weak a state. After a short stay Marie Bailly was therefore sent back to Sainte Foy. Her condition became continually worse, she was emaciated in an extreme degree, there was severe pain in the abdomen; Dr. le Roy considered her incurable and allowed her to go to Lourdes, with a certificate stating that she was suffering from tuberculous peritonitis.

'*The Pilgrimage and the Recovery.*

'" I do not know myself," said Marie Bailly later, " how the idea of going to Lourdes came to me. I had long since given up praying for my recovery. The first time the doctor told me that I was consumptive I felt most dreadfully hopeless; I was only twenty

H

years old and I could not resign myself at all to the thought that nothing could be done for me. One can be resigned to illness, to suffering, if only there is a gleam of hope in the horizon, but for me the only prospect was death and the grave. Gradually, however, I grew reconciled to my fate, I offered my life to God as an oblation : and, resigned to His holy will, I only awaited my dissolution. I do not understand how I conceived the idea of going to Lourdes.

' " I think it was one night in March when I was suffering most dreadfully. Then it was that I suddenly thought of Lourdes and I understood that I was to be cured there. My relatives were against it and the Sisters at the hospital too, as they thought the journey would be too much for me. But in spite of this I applied for a ticket and set off. I was carried to the train and laid upon a mattress ; I had to lie in a cramped position because the carriage was not wide enough to allow me to be stretched out.

' " The journey was extremely painful ; I had terrible pains in the abdomen and thought I should never reach Lourdes alive. The doctor stayed a long time with me in my carriage ; he asked me if I thought I would be cured, if I had faith in my recovery. I thought that the Blessed Virgin would surely help me, but, I added, she must hasten, for there is not much time left. During the whole of the journey I had no food whatever, not even a spoonful of tea." '

Thus far Marie Bailly. Her account leads on naturally to the doctor's notes : these also are given in Dr. Boissarie's book.

' Monday, May 26. In the train. A young girl

of twenty-two, pale, emaciated, with drawn features, lying on her back ; clothed in a black gown, instead of a belt a ribbon, which is fastened with a pin. My attention is immediately drawn to her very swollen abdomen, which I examine. On the left side there is a slightly more prominent place ; I find that there is a substance which resists touch. There is no fluid ; on percussion a dull sound.

' It seems that the abdominal cavity contains hard masses separated by a part that gives way under pressure ; it is an illustration of suppurative peritonitis. In view of these symptoms, the inherited tendencies of the patient and the history of her disease, as well as the diagnosis of so able a surgeon as Dr. Goullioud, I also presume the disease to be tuberculous peritonitis. Impossible to form any other hypothesis.

' The left side of the abdomen is very tender to the touch. Breathing rapid and jerky. Pulse 120. Œdema in the legs. The patient is quiet, there is no religious excitement.

' Tuesday, May 27. Lourdes. Arrival at 2 o'clock. The patient is brought from the train to the hospital. She is put to bed and is to rest until to-morrow. As a result of the journey her condition is worse. Vomiting, very violent pains. The breathing has become more rapid, pulse 120.

' Wednesday, May 28. In spite of the rest the patient is not better. At her own particular request, however, she is placed on a stretcher and taken to the grotto and the baths. She does not have a bath, has to be content with cold spongings on the chest and abdomen. At 10 o'clock returns to the hospital, where her condition causes grave anxiety. She is pale. The features drawn with pain, breathing very rapid. Weak pulse, 150. The face slightly bluish. Caffëine injection, hot fomentations, ice on the abdomen.

'May 28. 1.15 P.M. Condition very grave. The patient can only with difficulty and without real coherence answer the questions put to her. The abdomen very painful, very distended. Pulse irregular, very weak, hardly perceptible, about 160 ; jerky breathing (90), corpse-like face, very pale, faint violet hue. Nose, ears, hands and feet cold.'

At this moment Dr. Geoffroy, from Rive-de-Gier, joins in observing the patient. It is clear to him, as it is to his colleague, that the patient is dying. As she expresses a wish, however, to see the grotto once more, and as there is nothing to lose in yielding to her, she is carried down to it again. The doctor on duty continues the report :

' 1.50 P.M. The patient arrives at the baths. She is on her mattress in a state of apathy, stretched on her back, her head lying backwards, the face colourless, with a violet tinge in the cheeks. Very rapid breathing. The swollen abdomen is perceptible under the blanket.

' There is everything to gain at this moment and nothing to lose—and it is decided to take the patient to the baths and make a further attempt towards obtaining her recovery. Marie Baily's own account describes these moments.

' " A lady carrying my shroud walked behind my stretcher. Those who were carrying me prayed for my last moments. The doctor had said that carrying me to the baths would hasten my death and that I would return as a corpse.

' " I could not pray any more, but in spite of

everything I thought of the dear Blessed Virgin, and I was convinced that I would recover.[1] When I reached the wells they would not give me a bath, but only spongings. At first the water caused me terrible pain, and the ladies who were sponging me wanted to stop, but I asked them to go on. At the same moment I said interiorly to Our Lady of Lourdes, ' If thou wilt, thou canst cure me with this sponging just as well as with a bath.' " '

They continue the sponging, therefore, and the patient feels even more pain than before. It stabs her like knives, and suddenly all pain is gone. She sits up on the stretcher and exclaims : ' I am cured ! '

' She is out of her mind ! ' says the nurse.

They lay her down again on the stretcher and take her away. At this juncture the doctor resumes his account.

' 2.20 P.M. Marie Bailly is carried out of the *piscinæ* and set down before the grotto. There are not yet many people about and I can examine her at leisure.

' 2.30 to 2.40. The breathing is slower, more regular. The facial expression alters, a slight pinkish tint colours the skin. The patient seems to be better, and smiles to the nurse who is bending over her.

' 2.55 P.M. The outline of the body visible under the blanket is changing, the distended abdomen sinks

---

[1] It seemed strange to me that Mary Bailly, who is described as being in a dying state, should have been all the time so fully conscious as she is apparently supposed to have been, and it appears to me to weaken the impression of credibility otherwise given by this account.

Meanwhile, in Albert Eulenburg's *Real Encyclopädie der gesamten Heilkunde*, vol. ii. (Berlin and Vienna : 1907), p. 308, it is noted as a peculiarity of peritonitis that ' consciousness as a rule is clear, and it is not infrequently maintained up to the last moment.'

down. There is a marked improvement in the patient's appearance.

' 3.10. Hands, ears, nose warm. Breathing has become slow, 40 per minute, heart pulsations stronger, more regular, but still 140. The patient says that she feels better. She is given a little milk, which she is able to retain.

' 3.20. The patient sits up on the stretcher and looks about her. The blanket lies in slack folds over the abdomen. The limbs are moving, the body is turned round on the right side. The face has become calm and there is a faint tinge of healthy colour.

' 3.45 P.M. The patient is carried to the Rosary Church.

' 4.15. The improvement is pronounced. The breathing is slow, the face a faint pink. The patient tells me that she feels well, and that if she only dared, she would be quite able to get up. The change that has taken place is now so distinct that every one notices it. She is taken to the Bureau des Constatations ; she arrives on a mattress, she leaves in an invalid chair.

' 7.30 P.M. At the hospital. The patient is looking splendid. The face is very thin, but calm and faintly rosy. The breathing very regular. I examine her and find that the wall of the abdomen is now like that of a normal young girl of about twenty, soft, elastic, and bent inwards. Owing to emaciation the wall is very thin and this facilitates examination of the organs. I trace the aorta[1] with my finger ; on the right side there is in the depth a hard mass which

---

[1] The main artery, running from the heart down through the middle of the body.

is continued up to the groin. I can grasp with both hands round a very hard but not tender mass, as thick as a forearm and attached to the hindermost wall of the abdominal cavity. This tumour does not move after respiration.

'8 P.M. The improvement continues. The voice is stronger. Breathing 30, pulse 100, regular and vigorous.

'Next morning 6.30, Thursday, May 29. General condition excellent. The patient gets up for breakfast. Breathing 18, pulse 88. The abdomen quite normal. The hard mass observed yesterday has almost disappeared. There is a small, very hard, very firmly fixed, but painless tumour left.

'Friday, May 30. The patient has dressed herself and walks about in her room. She can walk upstairs. Her strength is returning rapidly. She can get into a carriage almost without assistance, and performs a journey of twenty-four hours sitting in a third-class carriage. She is very calm, is not in any state of religious excitement, avoids the curiosity of those about her as much as possible. Returns to the hospital at Sainte Foy.

'June 4th. Marie Bailly looks like a healthy young girl. Her appetite is good, she is increasing rapidly in weight, up to now almost a pound. The abdomen completely elastic, the tumour has quite disappeared. No sign of hysteria, no insensibility, no diminution of the powers of vision, no intellectual disturbance. Nor were any hysterical symptoms discoverable in her during her illness, no nerve attacks, neither depression nor excitement. She had an even and well-balanced mind.

'June 27. During the last fortnight Marie Bailly has increased twelve pounds in weight. She feels perfectly well.

'July. From and including the second week in July the legs are no longer swollen. The patient has made a complete recovery. She increases in weight at the rate of one kilo. (2 lbs.) per week. Her general health is excellent. The young girl is modest, quiet, rather intelligent, remembers well, speaks of her recovery only on being questioned, does not attempt to play the part of a saint.

'August 8. Marie Bailly leaves the hospital and enters the convent of Saint Vincent de Paul.'

With this the doctor concludes his notes on this remarkable recovery. Dr. Boissarie says in his book that on two later occasions Marie Bailly's blood was tested, and it was shown on serum re-actions that she had been tuberculous. There has been no relapse during the last seven years, and in 1909 Marie Bailly held an appointment at the orphan asylum at Pau.

Anyhow, one thing is certain, I reflect, as I put down the book. The contention of a Danish scientist in regard to Lourdes finds no justification here, in this accurate observation and record, and yet Dr. Lehmann maintains, in his 'Superstition and Witchcraft,'[1] that 'The recoveries at these places derive their miraculous character chiefly from the fact that no one ever takes the trouble to examine the patients and to determine whether there is really an organic lesion or only a disturbance of the nervous functions. The latter

[1] Alfred Lehmann, *Overtro og Trolddom*, vol. iv. (Copenhagen: 1896), p. 295 *seq*.

can be cured by psychic means, but not the former. While, therefore, a cure of nervous disorders is only natural and can be understood, the repair of an organic lesion would be a real miracle—but such a case has never yet been authenticated.'

I put aside the little sheet of paper on which I have written down, for the purpose of my notes on Lourdes, the unassailable opinion of this Danish scientist about things which *he* has apparently never taken the trouble to investigate.

Then the gong sounds for dinner and I go downstairs. The Belgians, as usual, occupy the middle table in the large dining-room. They talk and laugh, shout across the table, now in French, now in Flemish. And if I am not mistaken—no, it really *is* Julia Witthamer, the young girl who was cured yesterday, and who is now sitting here, not five paces from me. Her ulcerated stomach seems now to be a legend of the past —how she is enjoying her dinner! I see her partaking of roast veal and macaroni pudding, and drinking claret with this substantial fare.

Then there is a moment of silence in the room. The lame lady, who is usually late, comes in. But she does not, as usual, go up to her seat at the end of the Belgian table. Limping painfully and leaning on her crutch, she goes to Julia Witthamer, congratulates her, and with tears in her eyes kisses her on both cheeks.

XIV

I CANNOT tear myself away from Dr. Boissarie's book, and directly after dinner I go back to my room to resume my study of it. Every moment I stop at some account that is more remarkable than usual. There is plenty of material, as the bureau every year investigates and verifies about a hundred and fifty cases either of complete recovery or considerable improvement.[1] And yet it is by no means everything of this kind in Lourdes that comes to the knowledge of the doctors. A pilgrimage from Metz in 1905 had only reported two cures to the bureau, and there were, actually, twenty-two cases of improvement; another from Lyons in the same year had only reported five out of fifty-eight cases of cure and improvement. Dr. Boissarie therefore deals only with absolutely certain cases. It is amongst these that I am making a search, taking as my guide Dr. Lehmann's words: 'The cure of an organic lesion would be a genuine miracle, but such a case has never been verified.'

Organic lesion—an organic lesion—is a far ad-

---

[1] The average number for the years 1894 to 1903 is 157. The highest number, 236, was reached in 1898, the lowest, 103, was that of 1903.

vanced pulmonary tuberculosis, with cavities in the lungs—is that an organic lesion ? I wonder. If so, the history of Aurélie Huprelle might perhaps furnish the miracle required.

This young girl was cured on August 21, 1895, at seven o'clock in the morning by one bath in the *piscinæ*. In May of the same year her doctor had examined her thoroughly and found that—after six years' phthisis—a large cavity had been formed under the left clavicle, and that her condition altogether was extremely grave. She had recently had a violent hæmorrhage, and was only as a last, desperate resource allowed by the doctor to go to Lourdes. She was there cured completely by one single bath in the icy-cold water from the grotto, and on September 1, 1895, her medical adviser, Dr. Hardivilliers of Beauvais, declared, in a written statement, that all the symptoms of tuberculosis described in his earlier certificate had disappeared. In the winter of 1908–9, thirteen years after the cure, Dr. Boissarie visited Aurélie, and found that she had not been ill a single day since her recovery. People living in the district said about her, ' That is the young girl who had no lungs. Then she went to Lourdes and had a new pair put in ! ' [1]

[1] The following is the statement made by Dr. Hardivilliers (Boissarie, *L'Œuvre de Lourdes*, p. 280) :—

On April 20, 1895, I was for the first time called in to see Mademoiselle Aurélie Huprelle, living at Marais, in the Commune of St. Martin le Noeud. The result of my examination was as follows :

The patient states that she has had several attacks of bronchitis. At the present time she complains of severe dyspnœa, and frequent expectorations of blood. Coughs up large quantities in the morning. Perspires freely at night.

Percussion : Semi-dull sound at and under the right clavicle. The same, but more pronounced, on the left side.

Auscultation : Above right front and back surface raucous

But is this an organic lesion ? In the medical sense I suppose it is, and yet I feel, somehow, that Dr. Lehmann, like Zola's other self, the Parisian journalist in the novel 'Lourdes,' wants something external, visible to everyone, something like ' a cut finger that comes out of the water healed.'

So I turn over the pages in search of such a case. I pause for a moment at Joachine Dehant's cure of a large cancerous ulcer on the right leg, one of twelve years' standing. There are two certificates from the same doctor, one dated September 6, stating that the ulcer is there and ' covers two-thirds of the outer surface of the right leg,' another dated September 19, stating that the ulcer has completely disappeared, and that the place where it had been was only indicated by a faint reddish tinge on the skin. There are, moreover, numerous witnesses to the fact that the ulcer existed on the journey to Lourdes on September 12, a journey which would otherwise have been lacking in

breathing. On the left front and back surface sibilant breathing. Beneath the clavicle can be heard faint, moist rattling sounds ; also about the angle of the shoulder blade.

Over the whole extent of the lung pleural friction sounds. The patient's face is pale, emaciated, the epidermis discoloured, the nails domed.

Pulse rapid, 120 per minute.

Temperature up to 104 (39 Celsius).

The patient complains of complete lack of appetite.

* * * * * *

A month later all these symptoms have become still more pronounced, especially on the left side. An extended cavity has formed under the left clavicle. Respiration is distinctly cavernous. Moreover, other sounds can be heard, large-bladdered rattling sounds, friction sounds. The expectoration has changed—it is of the shape of coins, floating in a clear fluid, the so-called nummulated expectoration. The patient complains of pains in the chest, ' stitches ' here and there, most frequently underneath the shoulder blades. (*Cf.* Boissarie, *L'Œuvre de Lourdes*, p. 285 *seq.*)

motive, and that it had disappeared on the following day.[1] But this was in 1878, a long time ago. I look for something more recent. And then I stop at the recovery of Léonie Lévêque. It occurred in 1908, that is, only a year ago, and it is a case which has been exposed to the fullest daylight of modern medical science. I reproduce the history of Mademoiselle Lévêque's illness, such as it has been drawn up by Dr. Moullin, her medical attendant, and published by Dr. Boissarie.[2]

' Up to the age of fourteen the patient's health is good. Then a marked poverty of blood sets in and a curvature of the spine, which renders a surgical corset necessary. Since then Mademoiselle Lévêque is constantly more or less in bad health. At the age of eighteen she has appendicitis and inflammation of the intestines, and, in consequence of this, peritonitis. Condition extremely grave. Inflammation of the intestines is of long duration and special diet is necessary.

' At the age of about twenty the patient for the first time has pains in the head, attacks that last two or three hours. The pains are acute, localised above and in the hollows of the eyes. They end in a more or less copious flow of matter through the nostrils. These attacks occur at intervals of about three weeks. There is, moreover, constantly some headache.

' At about twenty-two years of age the patient suffers from cerebral anæmia, loses her memory, is unable to work.

---

[1] The documents relating to this case are to be found in Bertrin's *Histoire Critique*, pp. 526–537. The size of the ulcer (32 centim. by 15 = 12¾ in. by 6 in.) is given by Boissarie, *Lourdes* (Paris 1894), p. 266.

[2] *L'Œuvre de Lourdes*, pp. 20–22.

'At twenty-four she takes an engagement in a school at Honfleur. The sea air does her good, yet the attacks in the head continue. It is with difficulty that she teaches music.

'In June, 1906, œdema of the root of the nose; the patient consults a specialist at Havre, Dr. Lenhardt. He advises an operation, but being obliged to go away on a journey does not perform it.

'In September, 1906, the patient goes to Nogent-le-Rotrou and takes up a teaching engagement in Mademoiselle Renou's boarding-school. The pains in the head are less acute but still continue.

'In May, 1907, I am called in for the first time to see the patient. She has very violent pains above the hollows of the eyes, œdema of this part. Vomitings. As her condition appears to me to be grave, I advise the patient to consult Dr. Chevallier of Le Mans. He diagnoses the case as one of inflammation of the frontal sinuses.

'May 25. Operation. Incision above the arch of the left eye. Draining through the left nostril. As a result, an improvement lasting some days.

'June 17. Fresh operation. This time an open drainage is made, in the incision itself, one tube to the right and one to the left. No improvement, still very severe pains. General state of health poor, the patient cannot walk.

'July 8. Œdema of the frontal bone above the left eye. I again send the patient to Le Mans. Dr. Chevallier and Dr. Mordret state that an immediate operation is imperatively necessary, and on July 10 make an incision on the left side of the sinuses. Draining by means of gauze. During the first few days there is a slight improvement, then the pains return. The discharge of matter increases. The patient is still confined to bed, but lies on a couch during the day.

' Dr. Chevallier advises consultation with Dr. Laurens, who examines the patient and declares a new operation to be necessary. October 8.—Frontal incision to the right. The surface of the frontal bone is removed. Improvement while the draining continues.

' The general state of the patient's health is now very much affected. Severe heart attacks occur, complete loss of appetite, sleeplessness, dyspepsia, attacks of giddiness.

' November 14. Severe pains in the pit of the groin. I fear appendicitis, order ice. November 15.—Heart attacks, fainting fits. The patient is restored to consciousness by the injection of ether. Receives Extreme Unction.

' December 15. Condition almost unchanged, yet the patient is able to be moved to Paris, to her relatives. She is there given salt water injections. The forehead again begins to swell. She consults a specialist, Dr. Lacage, who advises an operation. She cannot resolve to consent to this ; again consults Dr. Laurens, who advises her to wait and to return to Nogent.

' February 11, 1908. Fresh incision and draining. On the 20th the patient is sent to the sanatorium at Pen-Bron, where she is attended by Dr. Poisson. As the pains continue she is given morphia injections. The heart continues to be very weak. The patient is sent to Pouliguen. The general condition improves, There is some appetite, but still sleeplessness. Discharge of matter through the nose and throat.

'At the end of April the patient returns to Nogent. The heart continues to be in a very bad state. I give her digitalis and spartein. The patient lies down almost all day. On May 7 she is weighed. Her weight is 44½ kilo. (about 6½ stone). Derangement of sight sets in, also attacks of giddiness. During one of these, on June 6, she falls down a flight of stairs and strikes her head; a boil forms. On June 16 Dr. Chevallier states that there is inflammation of the frontal bone, and that an operation must be performed, but the patient cannot bear either chloroform or cocaine. Two button-hole incisions at an interval of 3 centimètres (⅜ in.) are now made above the right eye-brow, and a canula is inserted through these openings. The discharge does not come until a few days after. The matter has an offensive odour, and flows in great quantities; it also runs through the nose into the patient's throat. The general state of health grows steadily worse ; the patient takes no other nourishment than a little champagne. The pains are so severe that the patient is given up to five injections of morphia a day. On June 12 the patient's weight has decreased to 41⅛ kilo. (5 stones 12 lbs.).

'The patient expresses a desire to go to Lourdes. I advise her not to travel in a pilgrim train, and she therefore goes alone, accompanied only by one of her colleagues, one of the mistresses in Mademoiselle Renou's school.'

So far this history, as written by the doctor. Now let Léonie Lévêque herself tell the rest. She wrote an account of her cure in the *Journal de la Grotte*, published in Lourdes, in the issue of November 8, 1908.

' It was in the month of April that I first thought of going to Lourdes, I dreamed about it in the night. . . .

' Towards May I talked vaguely to the head-mistress about it, but she pretended not to understand me, and I thought, " She will not let me go."

' On June 16 I was in Dr. Bonnière's private hospital at Le Mans, to undergo an operation. One of the Sisters there talked to me about Lourdes. After my return to Nogent I again spoke to the head-mistress, and this time she advised me herself to make the attempt. . . .

' But I continued to grow worse, and on July 11, after a dreadful attack, Dr. Moullin said : " I absolutely refuse to allow Mademoiselle Lévêque to go to Lourdes in a large train of pilgrims. If she wants to go, she must go alone, and as soon as possible ; in a few days it will perhaps be too late." I heard these words from my bed of suffering.

' On July 13, in the afternoon, Mademoiselle Renou came in and said that one of the mistresses was to go with me to Lourdes, and that we were to leave on the 15th. " Why not to-morrow ? " I asked. " Then I can be in Lourdes on the 16th, the Feast of Our Lady of Carmel." [1] " As you please," said Mademoiselle Renou, " I won't refuse you anything."

[1] July 16, 1858, is the date of the last of the apparitions at Lourdes. It occurred in the evening at about six o'clock. In commemoration of this event a Mass was said at the grotto, by special permission of Pius X, at *six o'clock in the evening*, on July 16, 1908. It was at this solemnity, which concluded the fifty years' jubilee at Lourdes, that Mademoiselle Lévêque wished to be present.

' Then the morning of July 14 dawned. I was deeply moved when I said good-bye to my colleagues. Was I not taking leave of them for ever? I felt very poorly, I had seen the doctors' certificates and knew how ill I was. . . .

' We left at 10.15, by way of Le Mans, Tours, Bordeaux. The journey was dreadful, every jolting of the train shook my poor suffering head. At Tours we had to wait two hours and a half, so that I was able to get a short rest there. It was July 14,[1] the town was decorated with flags, but I had no heart to look at anything.

' At five o'clock we left for Bordeaux. The pains were increasing and it became necessary to give me an injection of morphia. I could not bear either to lie down or to sit up.

' We arrived at Bordeaux at 10.30. I could not continue the journey, I was in too great an agony, my heart was beating violently, I was suffocating. We left the station and went to the nearest hotel. We had to go up three flights of stairs ; at every step I was obliged to stop and gasp for breath. Mademoiselle Aubert, my companion, had almost to carry me. The maid was alarmed at the prospect of having some one ill in the house and talked of speaking to the proprietress, but Mademoiselle Aubert managed to stop her.

' I had a terrible night, but hope returned with the dawn. We were soon to be in the city of miracles. I believed in my recovery, or at least in an improvement, and already began to make great plans for the future. My journey passed off a little better, and at a quarter

---

[1] The national fête of France.

past twelve we arrived at Lourdes. We put up at Madame de Salis', No. 6, Rue Garnavie.

' I wanted to go straight to the *piscinæ*, without resting first, in order to be present at Benediction of the Most Blessed Sacrament. I was in hopes that I should be cured, and I prayed earnestly.

' On the 16th I had the great happiness of being able to receive Holy Communion at the grotto. After that I went to the Medical Bureau to have my illness verified. I took with me the following certificate :

' "I hereby certify that Mademoiselle Lévêque, teacher at Mademoiselle Renou's school at Nogent-le-Rotrou, is suffering from inflammation of both frontal sinuses. In spite of several operations a cure has not been effected. Chronic secretion of pus continues, as well as the inflammation of the frontal bone. At the present moment no operation seems possible as the health of the patient is in every way very much weakened.   ' "CHEVALLIER, *Physician*.

' " Le Mans, June 9, 1908."

' I took with me a similar certificate from Dr. Moullin ; he particularly emphasised the weakness of the heart. Dr. Boissarie said to me, " Complete your pilgrimage and come back before you leave." [1]

' The pains now became more and more violent. At 4.30 I was placed in an ambulance and taken up to the Place in front of the Rosary Church for Benediction

---

[1] Boissarie says in his book (p. 19) : ' On July 16th, at four o'clock in the afternoon, Mademoiselle Lévêque came into the Bureau. Her head was wrapped up in several layers of flannel. The matter had soaked through her bandages, and several persons who were standing near her, especially Dr. Thomas, of Lons-de-Saulnier, stated that they had felt discomfort at the penetrating odour emitted by the ulcer.'

of the Blessed Sacrament. It was the great day, the solemn moment, but my sufferings were so severe that I was no longer able to pray. I raised my bandage for a moment, the discharge was flowing freely and emitted a sickening odour. Mademoiselle Aubert said to me, " I think the canula is slipping; but put on your bandage, it may be unpleasant for those standing near."

' The Sacred Host was approaching and stopped opposite my chair. Scalding tears were running down my cheeks. I stammered out, " My God! my God ! " I could not say anything else.

' The Blessed Sacrament passed on—and alas ! I was not cured. On the contrary, I suffered such terrible agony that I thought it must be death. All at once I had no hope any more, I only prayed to God to grant me resignation to His will, and comfort and strength to those dear to me.

' We were told that the sick would not be allowed to be present at the Mass in the evening. We then returned to Rue Garnavie and Mademoiselle Aubert renewed the bandage. It was soaked through; the matter had streamed out, not only through the canula, but above and below it. My companion wanted to stay with me, but I begged her to go to the evening Mass. In the meantime I installed myself on a little flat roof arranged like a garden.

' There was a clock opposite me. I watched its hands with feverish interest. I suffered more and more, the pains stabbed through my head, I did not know what to do with myself. At last I sat quite crouched up with my face in my hands and my head supported on my, knees.

' It was six o'clock—Mass was beginning. At

the same moment I felt an unutterable peace stealing over me. I felt that something stupendous, something divine, was now being accomplished. I began to weep uncontrollably, I could have run out to the grotto and thrown myself at Mary's feet. There was no pain at all any longer ; my sight, which had been double, became normal. And yet I did not say to myself, " I am cured " ! I was afraid of being mistaken. But I enjoyed the peace of that moment and thanked God for it with all my heart.

' I do not know how long I sat thus, but when I think of those wonderful moments my eyes involuntarily fill with tears. At last I ventured to touch my forehead. It did not hurt any more, even if I pressed hard, yet I dared not remove the bandage.

' At 7.15 the first people came back from Mass. There was a flight of stairs with fifteen steps at Madame de Salis'. I descended it without stopping to meet Mademoiselle Aubert. " I want to go to the grotto," I said. " I have no pains any more. I believe I am cured ! "

' It was impossible to reach the grotto. The whole town was *en fête*, decorated with flags and illuminated, very beautifully, I believe ; but I saw nothing, I was quite absorbed in my happiness. I went home again to go to bed ; I would not let Mademoiselle Aubert change the bandage, I was still afraid. . . .

' In the middle of the night I sat up in bed and exclaimed, " But I *am* really cured ! I have no pains any more, and I can lie in bed in any way I like." Mademoiselle Aubert now got up and I removed the bandage. The canula had slipped out and the whole of the right side of the forehead was quite healed. I put on a compress of Lourdes water and put on the bandage as before.[1] I had a good night but I could not sleep, I was far too happy. Next morning a little blackish blood came out of the left opening, but no matter any more. The canula could be inserted, but did not come out on the other side. I had no pains. I drank a big cup of chocolate and went on foot to hear Mass ; the walk did not tire me, nor did my heart give me any trouble. I went to the baths, and after that to the Medical Bureau. " My canula has dropped out," I told Dr. Boissarie, " and I cannot get it in again." " Then leave it alone," he answered. " Finish your pilgrimage and look in again before you go away."

' I ate a good dinner, had an appetite and was able to partake of everything, while for the last fortnight I had had nothing but water. In the afternoon I did some more walking ; I visited the Basilica, the Rosary Church, was present at the Benediction of the Blessed Sacrament. At half-past six I was back at my lodgings and wanted to change the bandage. The canula dropped into the wash basin. I tried to put it in again, it was impossible, my forehead was quite healed. From this moment there was no longer any discharge of matter, either through the nose or the throat.

' Saturday passed off quietly. The lady who attended to me at the baths was very much interested in what had happened ; she urged me to have it authenticated. But I was still afraid there might be some mistake.

[1] It does not appear from the accounts of this case that this had been applied all the time, but it seems probable.

LÉONIE LÉVÊQUE

' I did not go to the Bureau till Sunday morning. The doctors present noted that there was a slight depression in the place where the operations had been performed, but that all secretions, all pains, had disappeared, and that the recovery seemed to be complete.

' I went to the grotto, and on the same spot where Bernadette had once knelt down I said my Magnificat.'

The same afternoon at five o'clock Mademoiselle Lévêque left Lourdes. At Bordeaux the maidservant at the hotel recognised her. ' Was it not you, mademoiselle, who were here a couple of days ago and who were so ill ? ' ' Yes. And now I am well. I have been to Lourdes ! ' ' Ah, c'est chic, c'est chic ! '

At Le Mans the returning pilgrim visited the private hospital where she had been operated upon. There was great astonishment, every one wanted to see her. Dr. Chevallier exclaimed, ' But this is turning everything upside down ! Of course I will give you a certificate, but let us wait a fortnight first and see how you get on.' The joy at Nogent was boundless, everyone wanted to see Mademoiselle Lévêque and to touch her forehead.

This recovery has been maintained. On September 12, 1908, Léonie Lévêque made a pilgrimage of thanksgiving to Lourdes, and was then, at the *Bureau des Constatations*, examined by a large assembly of doctors. Not only was her forehead completely healed up and the former sore covered by a rosy scar, but her general state of health was improving. Mademoiselle Lévêque brought with her the following certificate from Dr. Moullin :—

' I have again seen the patient after her return from Lourdes. The scar formation on the wound is now complete; all that now remains is something like a small knob, but this is also about to disappear. The patient no longer feels any pain, either without exterior causes or from even very severe pressure. The derangement of the visual organs has ceased, as also the giddiness. The appetite is excellent; sleep also very good. The heart is again normal. Finally, the patient has, since her return home, been able to fulfil all the duties incumbent upon her without feeling the least weariness. On July 22 she weighed 39 kilo. 700 grammes; on August 14, 44 kilo. 400 grammes.

'MOULLIN, *Physician.*

' Nogent-le-Rotrou, August 18, 1908.'

XV

THE POWER OF THE SOUL OVER THE BODY—PSYCHO-
THERAPEUTICS AND SUGGESTION—CHARCOT AND
BERNHEIM—WHAT SUGGESTION CAN *NOT* DO—
THE FAILURE OF SUGGESTION AT LOURDES

I PUT down Dr. Boissarie's book ; I have hardly been
able to read the last lines in the fading daylight. It
is eight o'clock ; the Gave is foaming beneath my
windows, hurrying along under the trees where great
lamps are being lit. Above the basilica the mountains loom up—green close by, bluish grey further off,
under a cold, grey evening sky. I close the shutters,
light the electric lamp and resume, within my four
walls, in the closed and bright silence, my discussion
with the opponent I have brought with me from
Denmark, my familiar, modern science.

Very well, says this counterpart of myself, let all these
things be proved as conclusively as you and Dr. Boissarie
believe them to be. Let it all be perfectly correct as
regards Augusta de Muynck, and Marie Bailly, and
Mademoiselle Huprelle, and Joachine Dehant, and
Mademoiselle Lévêque. After all, they are all of them
nothing but cases of religious suggestion ; it is Charcot's
' Foi qui guérit ' ; it is the soul showing its power over
the body, and under a high pressure of feeling, an
exercise of all her powers, producing these wonderful
results.

To these remarks I make the following answer :—
To begin with, it is strange to hear a modern man
of science talk in this strain about the power of the
soul over the body. I could have understood such
words coming from the lips of a scholastic of the
Middle Ages ; *he* believed that the soul was a substance,
that it was the essential part of a man, that it was
even *forma corporis*, the principle that gave form
and consistency to the body.

But to all modern minds the soul is only one of
those old, somewhat cumbrous words, about which
Renan says that a quite new meaning must be put
into them before they can be used in their modern
sense. A psychologist of the present day uses the
term ' soul ' in the sense of consciousness, and
consciousness, again, is identical with all that it
comprises of imagination, feelings, movements of
the will, kept together by something called synthesis,
the nature of which no one can explain. In any case
synthesis is only something like a ribbon in which
a bunch of flowers is tied up. At death the ribbon
is untied, the flowers drop apart, fall to the ground,
wither, are trodden down, become dust, and cease
to exist. The soul no more has independent existence
than the tones of a harp. When the harp is broken
no music can ever again be heard from it.

That is the modern doctrine about the soul—
Höffding's, Wundt's, Jodl's, and whoever they all
are, these great men of our own day who occupy
the professors' chairs of the universities all over
Europe, and whose words are the creed of modern
humanity. This is the teaching of those who have
the public ear of the present day, and who are

responsible for their disciples. And their disciples go forth through their various countries and increase the responsibility of their masters a hundred and a thousand fold, and call out to the multitudes, ' Science has spoken ! You have no souls ! There is no immortality ! Hear it, oh, humanity, and arrange your affairs accordingly ! '

And you really mean to tell me that this poor soul, which is barely allowed to exist, this by-phenomenon of matter, as consciousness has been called by the French biologist and philosopher, le Dantec—that this soul is really possessed of such extraordinary powers ? That it can call the dead back to life, heal mortal wounds, heal in a moment that for which modern science has tried in vain to find remedies after years of effort ? Shame then, on our physicians, that they do not avail themselves of such wonderful powers, but leave it to the Catholic Church and her priests to make use of them to strengthen and spread abroad superstition. By means of these psychic powers, Lourdes alone effects at least one hundred and fifty recoveries in a year. And the cures thus effected are not trifles ; there are blind who receive their sight and deaf whose ears are opened ; consumptive, cancer, and tuberculous patients of all kinds who are restored to health and life. Millions of sufferers all the world over would be thankful if such things could be reproduced in other places.

And this has been attempted, answers my familiar, Science, in a superior voice. You mentioned Charcot just now, my dear sir, but you do not seem to know that both he, at La Salpêtrière, and Bernheim, at Nancy, have explained, and to a certain extent even imitated, the miracles at Lourdes. But, in a hospital in Paris, or in Copenhagen, one has not at one's disposal all the suggestive material possessed by a great religious centre. Your contention that the miracles at Lourdes ought to be imitated is therefore unreasonable and can simply be set aside.

Quite so, I answer. Now let us examine what Charcot and Bernheim think. The former, in his pamphlet ' La Foi qui guérit ' (1893), maintains that a miracle is a quite natural phenomenon, a result of the religious excitement produced by faith. He contends that in Lourdes ' only nervous ailments are cured. Everybody is agreed that when a crippled leg is cured, or a lame person regains the power to walk, this is done without any infringement of natural laws. As a set-off against this, a great deal of stir is made about tumours and sores also being healed—indeed, such cures seem to occur rather often at this place of miracles. Now, if it were to be proved that these tumours and these sores were of an hysterical nature, would not that make an end of miracles ? '

This contention would be of great importance if tumours and sores of hysterical origin were complaints of a fairly frequent occurrence. But they are so rare that Charcot does not quote a single case from his own practice, but is compelled to go back to the eighteenth century to find one. A certain Mademoiselle Coirin, he tells us, twice fell from her horse in the year 1716. Some time later she begins to be afflicted with various diseases, amongst others, nervous œdema, and finally a tumour develops in the breast. It opens and forms a sore, it is feared⸲to be cancer. Mademoiselle Coirin suffers from this trouble until 1731. Then a devout lady prays for her at the grave of the Jansenist deacon, Paris, who was renowned for his sanctity, and some earth from his grave is brought to the patient. This earth is no sooner placed on the ulcer than it begins to heal. It is, however, not quite healed until twenty days after, and six weeks elapse before the patient is able to go out.

This deacon, Paris, was, as stated, a Jansenist, and the miraculous incidents at his grave played a great part in the campaign carried on by Port Royal against the Ultramontanists and Jesuits. Meanwhile, provided the account of Mademoiselle Coirin's recovery is quite reliable, the miracle said to have happened is really not overwhelming. Many ulcers can be healed in the course of twenty days, and Mademoiselle Coirin, whose convalescence takes six weeks, has not much in common with a Marie Bailly, or with a Léonie Lévêque, who rises practically from the dead, eats, drinks, and walks. . . .

And this single case from an old book is all that Charcot can muster up against the recoveries that take place in Lourdes in full view of the twentieth century. . . .

Bernheim is the other great specialist of the present day in psycho-therapeutics. His attitude to Lourdes is friendly, condescendingly appreciative. ' All these observations down yonder,' he says, ' have been made by honourable men, and they have collected and tested them in the most complete sincerity. The facts are right enough, it is only the explanation that is at fault.' [1] The standpoint is the same as that of

---

[1] ' Toutes ces observations ont été recueillies avec sincerité et contrôlées par des hommes honorables. Les faits existent ; l'interprétation est erronée.' Bernheim : *De la Suggestion et ses Application à la Thérapeutique* (Paris : 1891, p. 296).

Alfred Lehmann. Quoting from Lasserre, he mentions in his book five cases of recovery from paralysis at Lourdes, besides one of nervous eye trouble and one of nervous hip disease also cured there. But these do not surpass what he is able to do himself in his cures by suggestion at Nancy.

These are the cases, then, that we must consider. In his book Bernheim mentions 105 cases in which his suggestive treatment has resulted in partly complete recovery, partly distinct improvement, either permanent or temporary.

There are, first, ten cases of 'organic trouble in the nervous system.' Of these, five are recoveries, three improvements, and one a relapse. Then there is a series of cures : eighteen cases of hysteria, twenty-seven of neuro-pathic complaints ; fifteen cases of various kinds of neurosis (St. Vitus' dance, somnambulism, writer's cramp), three cases of paralysis, four of stomach and intestine complaints (with three recoveries and one temporary improvement) ; thirteen cases of nervous sensations of pain which were more or less rapidly cured, nineteen cases of rheumatic trouble, and seven of various other complaints also related to the nerves.

Apparently, then, it is chiefly nervous complaints, or diseases originating in the nervous system, that Bernheim undertakes to cure.

It is the slowness of these cures that more than anything else distinguishes them from those at Lourdes. Suggestion has to be repeated again and again, from day to day, sometimes through five whole weeks. And the improvements he notes only occur gradually, very slowly, without the abrupt transitions peculiar

to Lourdes. One of Bernheim's most successful
cures is that of a young girl who had become crippled
as a result of years of rheumatic trouble. Aided by
the influence of continuous suggestion, Bernheim
gradually succeeded in making the patient lift her
arms above her head and stand on her feet. The
body, which at first collapsed when placed in an
upright position, was able after a time to hold itself
erect.

Again, suggestion can only be effective in the
treatment of functional disturbances. In a later work
Bernheim says that ' Suggestion is powerless to re-set
a limb that has been put out of joint, to cause
rheumatic swellings to disappear, or to restore cerebral tissue that has been destroyed. Do not let us
exaggerate. The influence of psycho-therapeutics on
organic injuries is limited. You cannot employ it to
remove an inflammation or check the development
of a tumour. Suggestion cannot destroy microbes or
heal an ulcer in the stomach, or put tubercles to
flight.' Not that Bernheim would decline to employ
suggestion in the treatment of tuberculous patients.
On the contrary, he endeavours with its help to
remove coughing, sleeplessness, and the like. ' By
means of this I strengthen the patient's power of
resistance against microbes and check, if I do not
arrest, the development of the disease.' But as for
obtaining the complete recovery of such a patient,
or restoring an organism that has been destroyed,
or in one instant ' putting in a new pair of lungs '
in a consumptive, or closing up an intestinal fistula,
healing an ulcer—with these Bernheim has no concern. ' One can only heal that which is capable of

being healed—suggestion cannot restore that which is destroyed.' [1]

The difference between that which happens at Lourdes and modern therapeutic suggestion is therefore fundamental. Several of the earliest cures at Lourdes might be explained by suggestion. As time goes on it seems that these cures decrease while the cures of organic ailments increase. Dr. Boissarie gives a striking example in his book of how *small* a part suggestion really plays at Lourdes.

' In the year 1897, during the great national pilgrimage,' he tells us, ' the Esplanade in front of the Rosaire presented a marvellous spectacle to all beholders. Fifteen hundred patients were seated or lying down in a double row all round the Place. The platform in front of the church was filled with three hundred and fifty people who had been cured in previous years and who carried a forest of gorgeous banners. Thousands and thousands of spectators waited in an indescribable suspense. Full of hope the sick gazed at the sound. It was like an electric current passing to and fro.

' Then Father Picard stepped forward and, with his commanding look, gazed on the multitude. Indicating with a gesture those who had recovered their health, he said to the sick, " Look, there are your models ! They were once what you are now. Do as they once did. Like you, they lay on their stretchers and they arose, stood up and walked. What is there to keep you back ? " And in a ringing voice of

[1] ' On ne peut guérir que ce qui est curable. . . . La suggestion ne peut restaurer ce qui est détruit.'—*Hypnotisme, Suggestion, Psycho-Thérapie* (Paris : 1903), p. 352. Previous quotations, pp. 321–325.

command he flung out the order over the sick, " Stand up and walk ! "

' His order was obeyed.   There were really invalids who stood up, left their stretchers and went towards the church.   There was general rejoicing, an irresistible rush of feeling swept over the multitude.   We are used to many things in Lourdes, but we have never been more deeply thrilled than on that day.   Some of the invalids stood up.   But how was it possible they did not all do so ?   How could even a single one fail to rise ? This rousing call, this emotion that stirred all hearts, these shouts that filled the air, and standing in front of the church, like a heavenly vision, those who had been healed, all this should have been enough to recall the dying to life and to make corpses rise from their graves.   It was impossible to attain to anything higher, we had reached the limits of human emotion. Religious suggestion had said its last word.'

And the result ?   The next day eight or ten who had been cured reported themselves at the bureau. They were those that Dr. Boissarie had seen rising on the previous day.   And they were : a consumptive woman, two patients with tuberculous abdominal inflammation, a woman with spinal tuberculosis, a man suffering from the same disease, one or two patients with pulmonary tuberculosis, one with chronic bronchitis and emphysema, finally three with nervous ailments.   *Three*—and there were *three hundred* nerve patients lying in front of Le Rosaire waiting to be cured !

The hypothesis of suggestion could not have received a more forcible refutation.

K

XVI

THE FEAST OF CORPUS CHRISTI AT LOURDES—THE
CANDLE-LIGHT PROCESSION—EVENING AT THE
GROTTO—A TALK WITH AN IRISH PRIEST—' THIS
IS YOUR HOUR AND THE POWER OF DARKNESS.'

I HAVE been in Lourdes three days and I feel as though
I had been here from time immemorial. I came
here from Italy—I had spent three weeks in Assisi,
Siena, Florence ; I had seen many things, had many
experiences—but it seems to have happened years
ago. Lourdes has its own strong atmosphere, there
is a sense of the supernatural before which everything
sinks into oblivion, making it recede far away and
deep down, and seem insignificant and unreal. Letters
from Denmark are brought to me, amongst them
there is an invitation to take part in a congress of
authors in Copenhagen. All these beautifully printed
programmes, syllabus cards, tickets of admission, look
so strange here in this town of miracles where man is
wrestling like Jacob with the angel—the wrestling
of faith on the highest summits : I will not let thee
go till thou hast blessed me !

I arrived in Lourdes on Thursday ; Friday and
Saturday are gone—the same pouring rain as on the
first day. Now Sunday morning has dawned in
radiant sunshine and the sky is a brilliant blue.

Below my windows the Gave ripples greenish-blue, no longer greenish-grey.

Later on the day grows warmer. The quivering leaves of the poplars glitter in the sun along the river banks and the firs stand motionless with branches like drooping banners. Up above Lourdes the mountains raise their green and sunlit heights—and furthest away in the south, in the direction of the sources of the river, the everlasting snow glitters on the high Pyrenees—on the summits at Argèles.

I go into the town where preparations are going on for the Feast of Corpus Christi to be kept to-day. Dazzling white sheets, covering both windows and doors and the show cases on the pavements, have long been hung up in front of the countless shops where rosaries and other objects of devotion are sold, and the owners of the shops are standing on steps and chairs fastening flowers and small green boughs on these white surfaces —as ermine is flecked with black spots. It is like walking through streets lined with flowered curtains. Box and myrtle are strewn in the middle of the street —freshly gathered branches and whole trees placed in tubs of water are ranged along the edge of the pavement, and altars, gorgeous in crimson and gold, with yellow candles and many coloured statues of saints, are set up at street corners and on market-places.

Besides the Flemish pilgrims, twelve hundred in number, who are still here, one train of pilgrims has arrived from Rennes and another from St. Jean de Luz at Bayonne. The two extremes of France meet here, Bretons and Basques, numbering respectively thirteen and seventeen hundred. They pervade the town dressed in their national costumes, and doing their shopping behind the white sheets amongst the rustling bunches of rosaries and the endless cases of jingling medals of all sizes, at all prices. Their purchases made, they all go down through the streets and congregate in front of the grotto, at the baths, or in the churches to hear Mass. It is possible from this day to gain some feeble impression of what Lourdes must be when one of the great pilgrimages fills the town in the height of summer, not with thousands, but with tens of thousands of people.

I go with the stream down to the Church of the Rosary. The Basques are singing at High Mass, the purest Gregorian chant, sung by the whole congregation, a choir of several hundred strong men's voices. ' Kyrie eleison, Kyrie eleison, Christe eleison,' rings out through the open doors. I pass on to the baths, to the grotto. The old Flemish women's white, winged head-dresses mingle with the black hoods of the Basque women. Yonder is a gathering of Bretonnes in white tulle caps. And what faces they have, framed in the white caps and black hoods—so pure, so regular, so noble ! Eyes whose glance has grown clear through centuries of gazing at the Crucified, and that have been washed free of all im-purities in the Precious Blood from the Sacred Wounds ; lips so calm and so pure—like a threshold over which the Saviour has passed again and again. . . . Perhaps, amongst these girls and women of all ages, there are some who can hardly write their own name, and whose only literature is their prayer-book—what does it matter when their names are indelibly written in the Book of Life, and when they have known how to shape their own lives like a work of art, like the finest poem, not on paper and in rhythms, but in reality and in deeds—

poems of goodness, affection, self-sacrifice, fulfilment of duty, and faithfulness unto death. . . .

More and more pilgrims are coming ; soon the whole space in front of the grotto is filled. The invalids, as usual, are lying on their stretchers or sitting in their ambulance chairs. And inside the grotto all the golden flames gleam and shimmer—the outer ones pale, the inner ones deep golden. The two great stands for candles look like two large illuminated Christmas trees.

Quiet reigns over this great crowd of people, all are praying silently. The rosaries rustle, behind us the river foams and rushes onwards on its swift course, a couple of twittering swallows dart swiftly to and fro over our heads. Then all at once the pilgrims, standing close together and pressed right up to the railing before the grotto, break into song, the song of the Breton pilgrims with the march-like rhythm so well-known to all visitors to Lourdes :-

Nous venons encore
Du pays d'Arvor
Où le sol est dur,
Et le cœur est fort.
Fiers de notre foi,
Notre saint trésor,
Nous venons du pays d'Arvor.

Gradually the singing increases in volume, the voices ring out around me, metallic and deep, the song of ' the strong hearts.' ' Proud of their faith, their sacred treasure,' they come from that province which is the tower of strength of Catholicism in France, that province in which Celtic depth of feeling and Celtic faithfulness keep knightly vigil over the ancient faith of Gaul and guard it against Latin pride of intellect and Frankish immorality.

On my way back to the hotel I see the door to the *Bureau des Constatations* standing open and I go in. There is a rather large gathering of people; doctors—Belgian and French—nurses, priests, visitors. I am already included amongst the habitués of the bureau; Dr. Boissarie nods to me across the table, and I take up a position in a corner from which I can see and hear while he continues questioning a patient.

This time it is a man, one Antoine van Deulen from Flanders. He is a cigar-maker, has been ill for thirteen years, suffering from an ulcer in the stomach, thinks he is cured now. He looks pale and miserable. His papers are produced, and it is stated in them that he has a tumour in the stomach as big as a man's fist. He explains that he feels no pain now—he has felt better during the whole of the journey, to-day he has even been able to eat meat. He is taken into another room to be examined; one of the young Belgian doctors is to examine him.

Marie Dillen, one of those who were cured on Friday, is also present. She is looking much better, says that she has a good appetite, and she now has round, rosy cheeks. On being requested to do so she tells us a little more about her recovery. She had to be carried to the baths, it was the fourth time. On being lowered into the water she felt nervous twitchings all over her body, and as soon as she was taken out she was able to walk, a thing that had been quite impossible for her for a long time.

' Let us see how you walk,' says Dr. Boissarie. The patient gets up, we make room for her, and smilingly she walks up and down a few times.

Evidently she still finds it difficult, however, and she is taken back to her chair.

Julia Witthamer is there too—there can be no doubt at all about the improvement in her. She has been weighed to-day and has increased one pound.

The Belgian doctor now comes out of the other room with the cigar-maker. Dr. Boissarie glances at him with a questioning look; his young colleague shakes his head. The patient who believes himself cured is then dismissed with the usual advice to try to eat, and then to report himself again. Then the meeting is adjourned and the bureau is closed. 'See you again this afternoon,' the old doctor calls to me as I go out. A few minutes later I see him strolling towards the town, his face inscrutable, meditative. . . .

The great procession of the Feast of Corpus Christi starts to-day from the parish church of Lourdes, the colossal but never completed work of the Abbé Peyramale. After dinner I go up through the town again ; it is now decorated all over. The church is crowded, and I work my way up through one of the side aisles till I am in a line with the choir. Vespers are nearly over—the Salve Regina rises up, borne by the flute-like tones of the boys and the strong, ringing voices of the men. And where could the words of the ancient hymn be more fittingly sung than here in Lourdes : Hail, holy Queen, Mother of Mercy, . . . to thee do we cry, poor banished children of Eve, to thee do we send up our sighs, mourning and weeping in this vale of tears . . . ' gementes et flentes in hac lacrymarum valle. . . .'

And yet there is nothing to-day that reminds one of Lourdes being a vale of tears, one great ' Hospital of the Seven Dolours.' Outside the blue summer sky and the white summer sunshine are bright and dazzling, and here, in the church, the chancel glows in colours like a picture by Fra Anglico.

Before the high altar, under the gorgeous Romanesque canopy, the three officiating priests in gold broidered vestments ; round about the steps, a group of altar boys in crimson cassocks, and crimson caps surmounting the small, brown Spanish faces with regular features and brilliant brown eyes. . . . Amongst them older boys in long sky-blue robes, carrying procession lamps ; and just outside the chancel screen the floor is like a garden of lilies formed by a troop of white clad little girls with white wreaths on their heads. In their hands they hold baskets from which they are to strew flowers before the Most Blessed Sacrament of the Altar on Its way through the town. A delicate blue veil of incense is drawn across the whole picture, the sunlight falls in broad slanting streamers through the high windows and the flames of hundreds of small candles glimmer like stitches of gold embroidery on a background of colours.

' All other feasts than those of religion are only mud feasts,' my friend, Father Willibrord Verkade, the Dutch monk and artist, once said to me. On his behalf and my own I apologise for the somewhat forceful expression. But no other festivals can really be compared with the festivals of the Church. For it is only in religious festivals that one has the feeling of bending before the Highest—before that which is indeed worthy of the festival.

I am very vividly conscious of this in the church in Lourdes, still more so when the procession, towards six o'clock, has reached the altar set up on the great platform outside Le Rosaire. The whole of the church façade has been arranged as a background for the altar and is covered with white and blue. A network of glow-lamps is drawn over it and, behind the forest of candles on the altar and the sea of flame from the procession, it shines like a huge jewelled setting of dull gold pearls.

All the invalids, Flemish, Breton, and Basque, are assembled with their friends on the esplanade. How different from yesterday and the day before, in the pouring rain! It is so warm to-day that the young Belgian girls, who are doing duty as nurses, are continually being called from stretcher to stretcher to give the invalids to drink—Lourdes water, which they pour from small blue and white enamelled tin cans slung in a strap over their shoulders. And in the golden light of late afternoon the gleaming monstrance passes round the Place whilst the supplications mount heavenwards.

' Seigneur, Fils de David, ayez pitié de nous !

' Seigneur, faites que je marche !

' Seigneur, faites que je voie !

' Seigneur, faites que j'entende !

' Lord, Thou Son of David, have mercy on us ! Heal my palsied limbs ! Open my ears ! Give me back the light of my eyes ! '

But no cure occurs during the procession of the Blessed Sacrament. It is carried back towards the church and a last Benediction is given from the altar on the platform to the kneeling crowds on the enormous Place. Nor are there now any that rise from their beds restored to health. The pilgrims disperse, and the mournful train of hundreds of stretchers and ambulances slowly forms into line and quietly and patiently returns to the hospital.

After supper I sit a while in the little garden belonging to the pension. Across the low wall I look along the river, purling and foaming, bluish-green, with bright, dark reflections, like liquid flint. Along the banks alders and firs and poplars stand motionless, and the tower and spire of the basilica are outlined against a background of green mountains lightly veiled in a thin haze. The furthest ridge fades away in blue, and closes the valley against the faint pink, milky evening sky. And far away in the south, far beyond town and fortress and the nearer mountains, I see glimpses of rose-tinted snow-covered peaks.

The beautiful day is succeeded by an equally beautiful evening, and at half past eight I am at the grotto. I go to the parapet above the river, and look out across the water. The hurrying waves of the Gave catch the last blue tints of daylight lingering amongst the grey and misty heights. Bats are winging over it. And up on the hills the trees stand ' clear cut against the light summer evening sky.

The pilgrims are assembling in front of the grotto for the torch-light procession—la procession aux flambeaux. Every evening during the visits of pilgrims to Lourdes this procession starts from the grotto, and passing up the ascents to the Basilica, goes down on the other side, to assemble finally in front of the Rosary Church, where the Credo is generally sung before the candles are extinguished. Consequently, every afternoon rows of candle-sellers may be seen at the sides of all the roads leading to the grotto, with large baskets full of white candles with blue rings, white and blue being the colours of the Blessed Virgin—and pilgrims provide themselves from these baskets. A small screen shaped like an extinguisher, to protect the flame from wind and rain, is sold with the candles.

The pilgrims gathered in front of the grotto have now finished saying their rosaries. All over the Place and along the parapet candles are being lit, they light up the dusky and still summer evening like a living bed of great golden flowers.

And look, yonder on the basilica, high up above the grotto, on the top of Massabieille, a few twinkling lights appear—the church is being illuminated, its contours are outlined with small golden glow lamps.

Down here, where I am standing, all the candles are lit and moving restlessly to and fro—like the dying sparks of burning paper . . . but soon they settle into ordered lines and like a luminous river the procession streams slowly out of the grotto, past the baths. At the same time the singing begins—a French hymn—of which I only hear the refrain, an endless, monotonous, unceasing ' Avé, avé, avé, Maria ! Avé, avé, avé, Maria ! '

How many people are there in this procession ? Twelve hundred, fourteen hundred, two thousand ? I don't know. I hasten on before them to the esplanade, and here I behold a new and most impressive sight. Not only the basilica is illuminated from the top, but the Rosary too, its enormous Romanesque façade below, and the immense rotunda of the dome above. A gigantic NLD flames in red and green from the middle of the tower of the basilica and electric projectors cast violet shadows over the slender spire. On the other side, towards Lourdes, a halo of glow-lamps gleams about the great Madonna statue on the esplanade, and high up, on the top of le Grand Ger, the mountain above the town, an electrically illuminated cross stands like burnished gold against a deep blue sky.

'Splendid indeed!' says a voice in English just beside me at this moment, and turning round I recognise a young Irish priest with whom I exchanged a few words yesterday at the bureau. His dark blue eyes gleam in the light of the illumination, and there is a look of enthusiasm in his firmly chiselled, very priestly face. We shake hands.

'Isn't it so?' he exclaims. 'You see such things as these only in the Catholic Church.'

And he points to the enormous ascents where the procession is now beginning to wind its way upwards. It is like a molten stream from a smelting furnace, little by little filling up a shadowy mould. The rear of the procession has not yet left the esplanade when the vanguard returns. The ascents to the basilica slant upwards like a colossal figure eight to the base of the church. And the singing goes on ceaselessly: 'Avé, avé, avé, Maria! Avé, avé, avé, Maria!' It is like a wandering people of singing flames.

The Irish priest and I take up our positions so that the procession must pass close in front of us when it comes down to the Place before the Rosaire. We recognise the members of the various pilgrimages—the Basque, Breton, and the Flemish. The light from the screened candles falls sharply on their open, singing lips, on the white wing-shaped head-dresses of the

Sisters of St. Vincent of Paul, on the hard and keen profiles of the Pyrenean peasants, and the glittering golden helmet, surmounted by a lace cap, of a Dutch peasant woman. At last they are all assembled before the façade of the Rosary Church, which shines in the light of its glow lamps as though studded with precious stones. From a corner of the platform I can look out over the thousands of candles ; in their coloured sugar-loaf screens they look like great tulips with waving stamens of fire. And amongst them all the light faces—a sea of countenances, all turned to one spot, to the shining white statue of the Blessed Virgin above the entrance to the church.

For a moment there is silence on the great Place. Then the singing bursts forth again and now it is the hymn of praise of the Blessed Virgin.

'My soul doth magnify the Lord : and my spirit hath rejoiced in God my Saviour.

'Because he hath regarded the humility of his handmaid : for, behold, from henceforth all generations shall call me blessed.

'Because he that is mighty hath done great things to me : and holy is his name.

'And his mercy is from generation unto generations, to that them fear him.

'He hath shewed might in his arm : he hath scattered the proud in the conceit of their heart.

'He hath put down the mighty from their seat, and hath exalted the humble.

'He hath filled the hungry with good things : and the rich he hath sent empty away.

'He hath received Israel his servant, being mindful of his mercy.

' As he spoke to our fathers, to Abraham and to his seed for ever.' [1]

The singing ceases, the candles are extinguished, the pilgrims quietly disperse. In company with the Irish priest I stroll slowly towards the baths. It is now a beautiful summer night, the sky is bright above the filmy white vapours of the meadows and the silvery blue water of the strangely living and swiftly gliding river. There are still many people praying quietly at the grotto, all the candles are still burning in it behind the closed gates—as they always burn, day and night, as they have burned without ceasing for half a century now.

The young priest and I sit down on the bench placed towards the Gave, facing the grotto. I tell him my thoughts of the afternoon about the Bretons and add a few words about the position of the Irish in the Anglo-Saxon world. Everywhere the Celts are the upholders of the Catholic Church—in France, in England, in North America——

' And in Australia, too,' the young Irishman breaks in. ' The persecution that England carried on against us, and which culminated in the Year of Terror of 1798, has in God's hands been instrumental in spreading the Catholic religion all over the British Empire. Amongst the English convicts in Australia there were many of my compatriots who had been deported because of their faith. At first an attempt was made to convert them by force to Protestantism, but when this proved unsuccessful the Colonial Government, in 1820, made the concession that two—*two!*—Catholic priests might be admitted to the country. Later on we

---

[1] St. Luke, i. 46–55.

were given entire liberty, and now, in 1900, Australia has over 700,000 Catholics with more than 800 priests, a cardinal-archbishop, four other archbishops, and fourteen bishops. We have thirteen hundred churches and a thousand schools with one hundred thousand scholars—it is a great tree that has grown from that small seed in the course of only eighty years.'

From ecclesiastical matters our talk strays into literature. I express my admiration of Robert Hugh Benson and of Sheehan.

'Sheehan!' exclaims the young priest. 'Why, he is a great friend of mine! When I am back in Ireland again, I will tell him that I met a Dane in Lourdes who knew him and had read his books.

'On the whole, we Catholics do not take at all a bad place in literature,' continues the priest. 'Here, in France, for instance, many of the most distinguished names are on our side : Paul Bourget altogether, Barrès, Lemaître, Léon Daudet, Charles Maurras more or less— and amongst deceased authors Verlaine and Huysmans still wield their influence.'

'You might add the greatest living writer of lyric poetry in France, François Jammes, and you might point out a similar movement in the world of painting, for an artist so decidedly Catholic as Maurice Denis—

'And yet,' I continue, 'and yet I don't believe in any revival of Catholic art. Catholic poetry, Catholic literature, must essentially be something that is born of the Catholic religion—as were the cathedrals of the twelfth century and the frescoes of the fourteenth. But those who are now called Catholic writers and artists—men like those you have just mentioned in France, or like Benson and Sheehan in England—are all converts, if not in religion, then in literature. They have had their training elsewhere, they have been the pupils of the great master novelists, and now they employ what they have learnt from them in the service of the Church.

'In other words, I think Catholic art has become a thing of the past. Protestant Christendom may still produce an art of its own ; we have excellent instances of this in Denmark. But Protestant Christendom is still young, only four hundred years old.

'The Catholic church has passed her season of flowering. She has flowered, in such abundance, such beauty, and for so long that the world has never seen it equalled, but now—— '

'Now,' the Irish priest interrupts me, ' now, you think it is the turn of *the others* to flower ? '

'Yes,' I answer. ' The world is a garden in which everything that mankind contains must put forth flowers and bear fruit for the Great Harvest. There are some words in the Gospels, in the story of the Passion, that have always made a deep impression on me. They are the words of Jesus when He says to His enemies, " This is your hour, and the power of darkness." I cannot but believe that we have now reached this hour.'

'You mentioned just now some modern French writers who have come close to Catholicism ; most of them, by the way, have done so for political reasons. But think of that host of highly-gifted writers who are consciously anti-Christian. Think of Anatole France, our great enemy, to whom all the cultured world of

Europe listens—think of the satirical, sceptical, sensualistic Rémy de Gourmont—or read one or two of the brilliantly written but wholly corrupt novels published by the Mercure de France.

'And in Germany, in Italy, in Scandinavia and Denmark, literature is developing in the same direction. Everyone who has talent enrols himself among the enemies of Christ. They are attracted to them as if by an elective affinity. Sometimes, perhaps, one or another has the strength to tear himself away for a time, partly or altogether. But they always return, if not before, then at the edge of the grave. It is as though they could not find peace till they had done so.'

'You are a pessimist, my dear sir! Benson, however, has said about the same thing.'

'I know he has. What I have said just now, I wrote in a small Danish weekly Catholic paper, already ten years ago. But the fact that the same line of thought forms the basis of your English *confrère's* wonderful book[1] has, of course, only confirmed me in my views.'

While we have been talking the Place has become almost deserted, only a few scattered faithful ones can still be seen, kneeling close to the railings of the grotto. The illuminations have been over for some time now, in their stead we have the stars shining over our heads. The Gave ripples and gurgles behind us in the calm of the summer night

'What is left, then, for us Catholics of the twentieth century, besides the crumbs that fall from the rich man's table?' the Irish priest at last asks bitterly.

[1] *The Lord of the World.*

L

For answer I point to the grotto, where the candles are burning steadily and gleaming out in the darkness of the night.

'This,' I say to him, *Magnum signum apparuit in cœlo.* 'A great sign appeared in heaven, a woman clothed with the sun, and the moon under her feet, and on her head a crown of twelve stars.'[1]

[1] Apocalypse (Rev.) of St. John, xii. 1.

XVII

NEXT to the *Bureau des Constatations Médicales*
is the *Bureau des Hospitaliers.* The door is standing
open as I pass by on Monday morning and I look
in. I see a great empty room, meagrely furnished
with a few office benches and tables. Papers and
open letters are lying in business-like disarray on a
desk, but I do not see any people about. For some
time I stand waiting, and meanwhile study a time-
table giving the following information :

THE HEAD MANAGEMENT OF HOSPITALITY OF NOTRE DAME DE LOURDES

Regulations for June 21, 1909.

Morning :

5.30 A.M.	The sick are taken to the grotto.
8.0 A.M.	The sick have breakfast.
9.0 A.M.	The baths open.
10.30 A.M.	The sick are taken back to the hospital.

Afternoon :

2.0 P.M.	The sick are taken to the grotto.
3.0 P.M.	The baths open.
4.30 P.M.	Benediction of the Most Blessed Sacrament.
5.30 P.M.	The sick are taken back to the hospital.

Superintendents on duty :
 Superintendent in chief : Comte de Beauchamp.
 Interior of the grotto : Colonel Marmet.
 Square before the grotto : M. Verhaven.
 The Baths : Rev. Father Espinos.
 Square at the Baths : Monsieur de Werbier.
 The Esplanade : Monsieur de la Salle.
 The Hospital : Monsieur Batkin.

Still no one comes who can give me the information I want, and I therefore go on to the Medical Bureau. I find Dr. Cox alone, and put before him my inquiries with regard to the organisation of the nursing at Lourdes. Who owns the hospital ? Who are the *hospitaliers*, the *hospitalières* ? What is the difference between them and the *brancardiers* ? Are they two independent bodies, and how are they recruited ? Who provides them with board and pays for their maintenance ?

With his usual kindness the English doctor enlightens me.

' To begin with the hospital, it is really incorrectly so called. It is a hospice, a home for the aged, belonging to the Sisters of Nevers, and they allow us the use of it during the season of the pilgrimages. We should not be able to use it if our sick did not live out of doors practically all day ; in the open air, at the grotto, and the baths, and on the esplanade. Now they only spend the night in the hospital and take their meals there.

' To look after all these invalids—you have seen these last few days how many there are, and this is only a trifling number compared with those that come

later on in the summer; for instance, during the great
national pilgrimage—we should require a whole
army of Sisters of Charity stationed at Lourdes. That
is, of course impossible. A confraternity has therefore
been founded, called the " Hospitalité de Notre Dame
de Lourdes," and consisting of ladies and gentlemen,
partly from France and partly from other countries,
who voluntarily place their services at the disposal
of the sick. The members of this confraternity are
called *hospitaliers* and *hospitalières* ; the men's and
the women's section each have a president, a vice-
president, and a council ; appointment to all these
offices is made by vote. *Brancardiers* is only a
distinctive name for those *hospitaliers* who are selected
to carry the sick from the station to the hospital, from
the hospital to the grotto and vice versâ. The ladies
are employed exclusively at the baths, where they
help in bathing the sick, in dressing wounds, &c. The
men's duties are more varied. They are sent by the
council wherever they are needed, to the railway
station when a train of pilgrims is expected, to the
piscinæ to bathe the sick, to the grotto to keep order
and be of use generally, to the hospital to watch at
bedsides. They are guides, bath attendants, stretcher-
bearers, day and night nurses, ready to do everything
they are told to do, at any time of the day or night.
Of course they do all this purely for the love of God ;
they are not paid even their expenses, but have to keep
themselves entirely.'

' And there is never any lack of them ? There are
always plenty to do this work ? '

' There are far more applications for admission
than required. The council can pick and choose.

Candidates are admitted on trial and wear a bronze medal the first year, and must by steady and unremitting work during one or more seasons prove themselves worthy of being finally enrolled in the confraternity. After that they are allowed to wear a silver medal and are then full members. At the present time there are several hundreds of them, and it may interest you to know that Dr. Boissarie and I are both entitled to wear the silver medal. The confraternity has its own chapel over there in the Rosary Church, and on certain days Mass is said there for our intentions.'

I express my thanks to the genial English doctor for his information and prepare to go. Dr. Boissarie has not yet put in an appearance, nor are there any invalids to be seen. Outside the dazzling sunshine of the morning, that seemed to promise another bright day, has turned into dulness and it is now beginning to rain. I put up my umbrella and stroll in a desultory way about Lourdes, in the oldest part of the town. Here is the Rue des Petits Fossés, where the Soubirous lived in 1858 ; their dwelling was part of the disused jail and was commonly called *le Cachot*. The street looks unpretentious, provincial ; one walks between grey garden walls ; an open door reveals some steps and green large-leafed fig-trees. The tops of acacias show above the walls.

In a small, narrow lane, running down from the Rue du Bourg, at the corner of the modern Boulevard de la Grotte, there is an old house with the inscription, 'Maison paternelle de Bernadette Soubirous.' The description is correct if it does give rise to erroneous ideas. The facts of the case are these :

When attention had been drawn to Bernadette and interest in her aroused, it could not fail to make a painful impression to learn that she and her family were living in such acutely distressed circumstances.

It was in vain that efforts were made to induce Bernadette to accept charity. Her parents were just as resolute. Estrade has preserved quite a number of small incidents showing the heroic disinterestedness of these worthy people, who, even in their direst need, refused to accept even considerable gifts of money. They could not bear the thought that the mission which had been entrusted to Bernadette should be in the very slightest degree tarnished.

Eight years passed by in this way and Bernadette's mother died on the Feast of the Immaculate Conception, December 8, 1866, in the midst of the most abject poverty. Not till then was the Abbé Peyramale allowed to reach out a helping hand. In company with the Bishop of Tarbes he bought a mill which happened to be for sale and handed it over to François Soubirous, who was thus enabled to resume his old trade on his own account. The family had, however, already left *le Cachot* in the Rue de Petits Fossés and had moved to the slightly better dwelling in the Rue du Bourg. And this is where the room that Bernadette once lived in may still be seen on the first floor. The chief piece of furniture is a large bedstead which has been surrounded by a railing to prevent visitors from chipping souvenirs from it. A few of the little seer's modest possessions, amongst them her white capeline, have been preserved here. On one of the walls there is a large, beautiful picture of Bernadette, a photograph taken in 1860. After being shown this room visitors are conducted into the adjoining house, facing the Boulevard de la Grotte, where a busy trade is carried on in objects of devotion, by Bernadette's youngest surviving brother, Pierre Bernard.

I purchase a few medals and other things and pass on—across the market-place, past the never completed, generously planned parish church, which the Abbé Peyramale had intended to be a sister church to the basilica above the grotto. The old priest lies buried in his unfinished church. He died on the Feast of the Nativity of our Lady, on September 8, 1877, and his death was the cause of perhaps the deepest grief known to Bernadette's heart. 'Oh, Father, Father!' she sobbed, weeping over the strict, good, fatherly Abbé Peyramale, who had at first seemed so stern and harsh to her and had since become her faithful friend and supporter. I pass by his house and garden now; it looks neglected and deserted; the gate is standing open to the forsaken paths, the gate that Bernadette timidly opened on that first morning when she came in from Massabieille with her message from the 'Lady.'

I return by way of the new Lourdes, and in a bookseller's window the title of a book catches my eye. It is 'Un séjour à Lourdes. Impressions d'un brancardier,' by Adolphe Retté. I purchase it and take it with me to my room, for the rain is pouring now. There is nothing to be done but to seek shelter as quickly as possible.

Adolphe Retté was at one time, that is about 1890, a symbolist writer who wrote in *La Plume*, and published small books printed on hand-made paper and in editions of a few hundred numbered copies. Then he disappeared from the literary world and turned up

in politics as an extreme radical, a revolutionary an-
archist—until he startled the world a couple of years
ago with a book on his conversion, entitled ' Du Diable
à Dieu,' in which he recounted his journey from the
desperate love of destruction and enjoyment of
extreme egoism to the sacrifice of self and the love
of all living things of Christianity.

' Du Diable à Dieu ' was followed by a so-called
' Catholic ' novel entitled ' Le Règne de la Bête,' in
which he describes the subjection of the individual in
Socialism. This book made the impression chiefly of
being a rough draft ; it seemed as though the author
had had other things in his mind while he wrote it, and
was in a hurry to finish it. And, as a matter of fact,
Retté had become more interested in religion than in
literature. The book about Lourdes shows it. In the
concise style of a diary he describes his pilgrimage
from Poitiers to Lourdes ; he made this journey on
foot, 260 miles, in twenty-four days, of which eight
were days of rest. Arrived in Lourdes he was, half
against his will, led to serve as *brancardier* and bath
attendant, and found this occupation so satisfying that
he stayed in it for two months. The impressions of his
activities during this period form the most valuable
part of the book.

' It often happens,' he says, ' that in the course of
a couple of hours one has to give baths to four or five
hundred invalids. Many of them are so infirm or
so crippled that they cannot help themselves. There
is many a pair of boots to pull off and many a flannel
vest of doubtful cleanliness to remove. There are
palsied men who have to be put in straps or laid on
boards before they can be lowered into the water. It

takes four, six, sometimes eight people to do it, the main thing is that it *is* done. And then the care that is necessary not to hurt or scratch these poor, tortured bodies, that feel in agony at every movement.

' Here may be seen a former government official busy putting on a bandage. There is an engineer helping a cancer patient to get dressed. In the next cubicle a manufacturer is engaged in fishing cotton wool and bandages out of the bath ; a stalwart soldier is carrying the most afflicted ones away in his arms or on his back. And right through it all one goes on praying.'

In a few rapidly-drawn lines Retté sketches some portraits of his comrades at the baths.

' There is M. de Barbarin, a man of sixty ; he is a specialist in putting bandages on again. I have seen him standing five or six hours at a time, bending over boils and ulcers, without ever showing signs of weariness or disgust. Yonder is the Abbé Blanchet, who has a particular affection for cancer patients, those who are afflicted with lupus, and those who are almost half dead. . . . Berton, a sturdy peasant from the Charente Inférieure ; he was cured last year, and has now come back this year to show his gratitude. . . . Henry Noury from Nantes, who had himself an ulcer on the leg, but forgot it in helping the others. Harmois, a feeble, old priest from Paris, but the first to come and the last to go.

' A warm friendship bound all these different people together. The happiness of working together in the service of the Blessed Virgin created bonds between us that nothing could break. We were often asked whether we did not, after a time, feel sickened amongst all this suffering and these ceaselessly repeated groans. I answered, on my own account: "By no means. To me it is as if I had heaven enshrined in my heart."

'After all, it is only thinking too much about one's self that makes one sad. If you have once succeeded in pushing back that ever-complaining self and in making it give way to others, and besides this allowed yourself to be guided by the grace that speaks so distinctly during the work at the baths, you become quite changed, and you are surprised at being able to do work that you would before have shuddered at thinking about.'

And as this applies to those who wait on the sick, it applies, too, in a great measure, to the sick themselves. 'Instead of being impatient for their turn to come,' says Retté, 'the sick mutually call attention to one another—"He is more miserable than I, let him go in first." And they try to help one another in undressing, they encourage one another, pray for those who are in the baths, forget their own sufferings in those of others.' As a particularly pathetic incident Retté relates the following case:

'Amongst the pilgrims from Les Landes there was a peasant of about fifty years of age. He was completely paralysed, and, moreover, covered with suppurating sores of an offensive odour all over his body. It took six of us to lay him on a plank and lower him into the water. He showed great patience and much resignation to God's will, and we came to have a liking for the man. For three consecutive days he was bathed without the least result. His faith remained unshaken; indeed, it seemed as though disappointment only made it more ardent. On the evening before the day when he was to leave he was allowed to spend the night in prayer at the grotto, in company with the young *brancardier* who had charge of him.

'Next morning he came and had his bath as usual. It was the last, and it did him no more good than any of the previous ones. But his calm face showed no trace of discouragement, there was a quiet radiance in his eyes. We crowded round him and reminded him that cures have often occurred on the way home from Lourdes, nay, even later.

'"No," he answered, "I shall not be cured. During the night I prayed to the Blessed Virgin to let me keep my sufferings. I have offered them to God in propitiation for all the sins committed in the parish at home, where most of the people are unbelievers. I felt that my prayer was heard. So don't pity me. I am quite happy."'

Retté also notes one or two significant details in connection with the voluntary nurses, the *hospitalières*. Some of them save up money for a whole year in order to be able to make the journey to Lourdes and spend their holidays in tending the sick. Others are wealthy and belong to great families. These leave to their relations the pleasures of fashionable Biarritz and themselves go instead to Lourdes. 'It is now the third time that my people have written for me to come,' one of these young ladies told Retté, 'and for the third time I have had my trunk packed to go to Biarritz. But then, when I get down to the hospital to say good-bye to my invalids, I can't help it—I go back and unpack again. One forgets one's self in Lourdes.'

Self-forgetfulness, that is the constantly recurring word when Retté wishes to sum up his impressions in one main thought. And it is evident, from a little sketch that he gives of a night spent in the hospital, and of the following morning, that he has himself experienced this self-forgetfulness and the happiness it gives.

'One night,' he says, 'there was a cancer patient from Nancy in one of the wards. The Sisters of St. Vincent at Montrouge had recommended him to me. He had an ulcer below the navel, that was continually suppurating and emitting a penetrating stench. His state was extremely grave and death might come at any moment. In order that his wife, who had come with him, might get a little sleep, I offered to stay beside him.

'The ward was crowded that night. The beds were ranged so close together that it was hardly possible to move between them. It was very warm and all the windows were open.

'During most of the time I sat at the head of my cancer patient's bed. We said the rosary when his pains had somewhat abated. Now and then he fell asleep, and I went about in the ward seeing to the wants of the other patients.

'Towards dawn it suddenly grew cool. Complaining voices asked for the windows to be closed. I complied. But the odour from the cancer patient, from the tuberculous, from the many with open sores, in addition to the other exhalations in the ward, became so unbearable that I felt as if I were being suffocated. I snatched up my bottle of eau de Cologne, but it was of no use, even that seemed to smell of cancer.

This corpse-like smell was actually so penetrating that even after three days I could not get it out of my nose, and the clothes I had worn retained the smell a long time. I was on the point of being sick when I was at last relieved from duty and could go out in the fresh air.

'I went down to the courtyard of the hospital and drew in deep breaths of the fresh morning air. The day was dawning, the Cross on the Grand Ger glowed in colours of rose and gold, a last star quivered in the pallid blue sky. There was no sound but the foaming of the river in the cascades close by, near the convent of Poor Clares.

'And then it seemed as though a luminous joy streamed down upon me. I was filled with a deep and peaceful happiness, with a clearness that penetrated to the innermost recesses of my soul. I was happy, cheerful, and contented ; something was ringing in my heart, in tones of crystal clearness.

'Instead of going home to bed I wandered down to the grotto. The man who attends to the candles opened the gate for me and I knelt down behind the altar. A silence of wordless prayer descended upon me, and thanksgiving and love mounted from my soul like great resplendent roses. . . .'

XVIII

IT is the last day of the Belgians at Lourdes, they go away to-morrow. Apparently in order to test their steadfastness once more, the sky opened up all its sluices at about four o'clock, and they received Benediction of the Blessed Sacrament under a downright shower bath. As wet as a drowned rat, I leave the esplanade and go back to my room, where I change into dry clothes.

And while the rain is pouring down over the bottle-green Gave, I resume my silent combat, within four walls, with my adversary, sceptical science.

Let Bernheim say and think what he likes—let him be unable to imitate the miraculous cures at Lourdes—after all, when all is done, it must be faith that cures; suggestion, illusion, the fixed idea, that works.

This, it seems to me, expresses the views of the scientific *quand même*. And so it is ardent faith, firm conviction, that arrests tuberculosis, heals inflammation, and causes even the most dangerous and long enduring sufferings to cease, as in the cases of Augusta de Muynck, Léonie Lévêque, and so many others whose diseases are recorded in the ' Annales de la Grotte.'

Meanwhile, what becomes of this hypothesis if

it can be shown that it is by no means all of those who recover their health who are possessed of that ' faith that moves mountains,' spoken of in the Gospels ? As it happens, this was the case with Mademoiselle Lévêque. It is true that up to her fifteenth year she had received a Catholic education in the pension of the Dames du Sacré Cœur. But then she was placed in other environment, read modern books, and became quite unbelieving. The Catholic doctrine of the Blessed Sacrament seemed to her particularly unreasonable ; and during a stay in England an increasing aversion for this belief took firmer root in her mind. She had heard of Lourdes only through Zola's novel.[1]

Then her illness began, and under its influence Mademoiselle Lévêque regained a faint sense of religion, especially a belief in a Supreme Being. It was only by slow degrees that she found her way back to Catholicism, and she knew nothing of the part that the Blessed Sacrament of the Altar plays at Lourdes until she went there herself. It was, therefore, not any deep or earnest or firmly grounded faith that worked here. And yet the result was considerable, an inflammation that several operations had failed to cure was, so to speak, removed in a moment and removed permanently.

A still smaller modicum of faith was that possessed by a blind man from Lille, one Kersbilck, who received his sight at Lourdes on September 17, 1908. Kersbilck was a working man, and it is a well-known fact that the religious sense is not the strong point of French working men. A' Sister of Charity had persuaded

[1] *Journal de la Grotte*, September 12, 1909.

him to go to Lourdes, but he did not give any actual proof of understanding what was going on about him. He spoke of the *braconniers* (poachers) instead of *brancardiers*, and in connection with the bath houses or *piscinæ* he used a word that was not exactly respectful. His medical certificate stated his case as one of complete blindness caused by atrophy of the visual nerve. This man regained his sight at Lourdes, and on his return to Lille was given an uproarious reception by more than a thousand working men, most of them Socialists, who had assembled at the railway station, and some of whom asserted that Kersbilck had accepted bribes to pretend that he was cured.[1]

But the typical case of a patient who comes to Lourdes without faith, who is even at enmity with religion, yet who is completely cured there, is that of Gabriel Gargam. This is his story : [2]

It was the evening of December 17, 1899. The express that leaves Bordeaux at 10.30 had started, and Gabriel Gargam, postal assistant, was at his work in the mail van, the last carriage but one in the train. Between Bordeaux and Angoulême the train slackened speed ; the engine was in a bad condition, and although the driver made every effort to keep up the regulation speed it was impossible for him to do so. At Livernant, some few kilometres from Angoulême, he could not make the train go any further; the engine stopped. Ten minutes after, the express, however, the *rapide* from Bordeaux to Paris, was due. 'We had hardly stopped, therefore,' Gargam said later, 'when a terrible, dull sound could be heard approaching with

---

[1] Boissarie, *L'Œuvre de Lourdes*, pp. 195–202.
[2] *Ibid.*, pp. 93–109 ; Bertrin, *Histoire Critique*, pp. 330–357.

M

the speed of lightning; it was the *rapide*, running at a speed of over fifty miles per hour. Owing to a curve on the line, it was impossible for her driver to catch sight of us before it was too late.

 ' It was half-past twelve. Hardly more than a few seconds passed before we were shattered and the carriage splintered into match-wood. My comrades and I were flung in all directions; I was thrown thirty yards away and fell to the bottom of a snow-drift.

' All my recollection stops at that terrible sound of the train that was rushing to our destruction. It was such a frightful shock to my nerves that in a certain sense I ceased to exist from that moment.

' We were four postmen in the train. One of us was killed and two others are invalids to this day. As for me, I lay buried in the snow until I was found the next morning at seven. I was taken to the hospital at Angoulême with the other injured. And in what a state! I was one mass of injuries and could not move a limb. I did not recover consciousness until towards evening. For the first fortnight I could take no other food than the juice I sucked from slices of orange.

' On January 1 I had improved so far that I could eat an egg, but my food was still only of the slightest. I ate enough not to die of starvation, not enough to regain strength. The doctors soon found out that I was completely paralysed from the waist downwards. Moreover, I could not lift up my head, and vomited at the least movement.'

Dr. Decressac, physician at the hospital at Angoulême, tried to effect an improvement in the condition of the patient by means of baths. They only made matters worse, however ; the throat contracted so that the patient could no longer swallow anything at all. It became necessary to feed him by means of a tube, and even this could only be inserted once a day.

Eight months after the accident—in August 1900—Gargam was still lying in this condition. The young man, who had by nature been sound and robust, gradually became like a skeleton: round the calf he measured only nine inches ; the thigh, measured round the middle, was only ten. His weight was 36 kilo. (72 lbs.)

Gargam had claimed compensation from the Paris-Orleans Railway Company and had won his case in two instances. In the first, the court gave the following reasons for supporting his claim :

' Gargam will require at least two persons in constant attendance upon him, and they must be competent enough to give him, day and night, the special nursing necessary to him in order to preserve his life ; he will, moreover, frequently need medical attendance, this accident having changed him into an absolute wreck of a human being, whose intelligence alone remains intact.' [1]

The court had ordered the railway company to pay Gargam an annuity of 6,000 francs and a compensation once for all of 60,000 francs. The Company appealed to the higher court at Bordeaux, but only with the result that the judgment was confirmed.

---

[1] ' Une véritable épave humaine, dans laquelle l'intelligence seule n'a pas été atteint.'   Bertrin, *Histoire Critique*, p. 338. *Idem*, pp. 544–549, for medical certificates and legal papers relating to the case.

This happened on July 2, 1901, and Gargam's future was so far assured.

But what a sad future ! And was there indeed any future ?

The doctors did not hold out much hope. Gargam still had a feeling of intense pain about the lumbar vertebræ, and it was the opinion of the under-surgeon at the hospital, Dr. Teissier, that the spinal column had been dislocated in the lumbar region, and that Gargam's paralysis was due to the pressure thus caused on the marrow. Teissier therefore suggested trepanning the spine, but the operation was not performed as the patient strongly objected to the idea.

Then one day bluish black spots appeared on the patient's feet. Gangrene had set in, and it seemed as though Gargam, while still alive, would see the beginning of his own dissolution. An iron cradle was placed over the lower end of his bed, to prevent the sheet from coming into contact with the putrefying flesh.

And so Gargam lay and waited for death. His mother, who lived in Angoulême, came to see him every day ; she was a devout woman and often tried, but always in vain, to speak of religion to her afflicted son. The chaplain at the hospital was just as unsuccessful. For fifteen years Gargam had had nothing to do with the Church, nor did he now wish for her help.

He knew he was in a hopeless state, and that at the best he might drag along this dreary existence a few summers and winters yet. He was only thirty-one, had done well in the postal service and his prospects had been excellent. Now it was all wasted, irretrievably lost, destroyed in one single terrible moment, and only because an engine-driver had not taken care to have his engine in proper working order. Was death or life, happiness or disaster, to depend on such trifles as these ? And yet, in spite of this, there were people who believed in a Providence !

Gargam was more embittered than ever against religion, and more impervious to its influence. If one of the Sisters at the hospital came in and began to pray for him at his bedside, he was irritated and annoyed.

And yet he did not seem unwilling to listen when his mother one day timidly suggested that he should try Lourdes. Dr. Teissier had again spoken to him about trepanning, and Gargam could not bear the thought of having to go through this new and great suffering. Besides, he had now been lying ill in this hospital for twenty months, and had grown tired of looking every day at the same white ceiling. Going to Lourdes meant getting away into new surroundings. And if he was to die he might as well die there, where he would at least be with those who were dear to him, where his mother would be with him.

Gargam discussed it with a cousin who was a doctor, and the journey to Lourdes was decided upon. His mother, who had already succeeded in this, now became bolder and explained to her son that if the pilgrimage was to be of any help to him, he must first be reconciled to God, that is to say, make his confession and receive Holy Communion. Gargam was quite willing to please his mother; besides, if one was a pilgrim, evidently one must act like a pilgrim ! He was going to perform an experiment, he must therefore carry out all the details connected with it. He agreed to making his confession, and, after some demur and an attempt at procrastination, also to receiving the Blessed Sacrament. There were great practical difficulties, however, in administering this, as he could hardly swallow anything. He succeeded, though, in swallowing a quite small particle of a Host.

On August 19, 1901, the departure for Lourdes took place. A stretcher of the width of a carriage door had been made for him; here, too, a cradle kept the sheet up from the gangrened feet. A male nurse and three other persons accompanied him.

The journey was extremely painful, Gargam fainting on the way. As they were approaching Lourdes, on the morning of August 20, his mother showed him the great crucifix that can be seen from the top of the Mont des Bretons, far out in the country, proclaiming to the pilgrim that he is near the goal of his journey. Gargam turned his head away, unwilling to look at it, and refused to take any part in his mother's prayers.

Yet, in spite of this mood of antipathy against religion, he received Holy Communion an hour later at the grotto. He had promised his mother that he would; besides, it was part of the pilgrimage, of the cure!

And now something happened that is quite inexplicable on all hypotheses of suggestion, because there is such an absolute lack of proportion between cause and effect—between Gargam's somewhat supercilious yielding to that to which his friends ascribed so much importance, and which after all could not do him any harm—and the consequences of his yielding.

For he had hardly received the Sacred Host before he was overcome by a great desire to pray. And yet he could not formulate a single prayer, could not, in fact, utter a word—it was as though he was being suffocated, he gasped for breath and at last burst into tears—he felt as if light was being poured into his soul from on high—he *saw*, and he *believed*. With a feeling of boundless trust, of deep confidence, he turned his tear-dimmed eyes to the statue of Mary in the niche above the grotto.

It was that which Christianity calls Grace that was streaming into Gargam's soul. Many prayers had lately been said for his conversion—one of his aunts was a nun at the Sacré Cœur, a cousin was a Poor Clare at Orthez—and while the sick man gazed steadfastly, ecstatically up at the image of the Blessed Virgin, the light grew clearer and clearer within him, that light by which one sees with almost physical distinctness that everything that Christianity teaches is really true, that God is in His Heaven, that Jesus was God and is God, and that in Him is peace, salvation, and everlasting life.

Gargam had become a believer. But he was not cured. He could not leave his stretcher, and had to eat his dinner by means of a tube.

And it seemed as though he were not to be cured. In the afternoon he was carried to the baths and lowered into the water on a plank. He succeeded in praying; he repeated the prayers of the attendants : ' Our Lady of Lourdes, heal our sick ! Health of the sick, pray for us.' Nothing happened.

At four o'clock in the afternoon he was taken to the esplanade to receive Benediction. He fainted there, worn out with the exertions of the last twenty-four hours. He was believed to be dead, and his attendants were about to cover his face.

Then he opened his eyes, thought at first that all was over, and was filled with deep disappointment. He then heard the supplications and prayers going on around him. And suddenly he tried to raise himself on his elbows—sank back—again tried to rise. They tried to keep him down, but he protested: ' You ought rather to help me,' he cried in a hollow voice. And, suddenly he stood upright, tall, gaunt, wrapped in his long night-shirt, like a skeleton in a shroud. He walked five tottering steps towards the monstrance with the Blessed Sacrament. Then he stumbled, was caught as he fell and led back to his bed.

At this moment there were thirty thousand people gathered in front of Le Rosaire, and Gargam's stretcher was all at once the focus of everyone's gaze, the centre of the eager interest of all. The invalid now made whole was again stretched on his bed ; great tears were rolling down his emaciated cheeks, and again and again he exclaimed, ' Holy Virgin, I thank thee ! ' His mother knelt beside him, and between her sobs she stammered, ' It is twenty months since he was last able to speak aloud ! '

· ' Gargam's appearance at the *Bureau des Constatations*,' says Dr. Boissarie, ' was one of the most impressive sights I had ever witnessed. It was during the National Pilgrimage, and over sixty doctors were present in the bureau—hospital surgeons, professors, doctors from abroad.

' Gargam arrived on a stretcher, wrapped in a long night-shirt, attended by his mother, his male nurse, and several ladies from the hospital. He stood up; we beheld a ghost.

'Great staring eyes were all that lived in this emaciated, colourless face; he was bald and looked like an old man, yet he was only thirty-two. There was great excitement and a hail of questions. We were compelled to put off the examination till the next day, we could not have kept the crowd from the doors of the bureau.

'On the following day it was impossible to find room for all the doctors in the bureau. People stood on chairs and benches in order to see. Gargam walked in, he was not carried, and he was correctly dressed in a new suit of clothes, bought for him the previous evening. The sores on his feet, suppurating freely the day before, were about closed up; he could walk without too much difficulty. He gave a very clear account of his recovery, and said that the previous evening he was able to put away the tube and to eat like other people. He had eaten soup, oysters, the wing of a chicken, and a bunch of grapes. He had had an excellent night. He was very thin; it was a skeleton that stood before us.

'One of those present asked him about his religious convictions. Gargam answered, "As late as the day before yesterday, when I left Angoulême, I was a sceptic and did not believe in miracles. Nay, even yesterday morning I did not believe in them."'

Gargam stayed some time in Lourdes after his recovery. He increased rapidly in weight, a little over twenty pounds in a few days; the muscles filled out too, he soon measured twelve centimètres ($4\frac{1}{2}$ in.) more round the thigh than before August 20. And this man, who only lately was dying, developed an astonishing power of endurance, submitting to the questions of the curious, the examinations of doctors, all day long. It was simply a case of resurrection. As it was said of Lazarus it might also be said of Gargam, ' by this time he stinketh.'

This man, who was actually at the edge of the grave, and was in one instant restored to life, has during the years that have elapsed since then enjoyed excellent health. It was proved by a Röntgen ray examination that Dr. Teissier was right in his conjecture, in so far as the spinal column was still dislocated in the lumbar region. This fact notwithstanding, the paralysis was cured and the gangrene in the feet disappeared completely.

Gargam returned to his employment in the postal service. After his recovery the Paris-Orleans Railway Company withdrew his annuity and he was again obliged to work for his living. But every year during the month of August Gargam comes to Lourdes and helps at the baths as *brancardier*. That is his way of giving thanks for his recovery.

Thus the history of Gabriel Gargam, told by trustworthy men. Retté saw him here in Lourdes last year and questioned him. . . . And now, Science, my familiar friend and compatriot, what do you think of this ?

I get up and go to the window. It is nearly eight o'clock and growing dark, and the rain is still pouring. And what is this ? Yonder, in front of the grotto and the baths ? Surely those are candles that I see moving to and fro. No, not candles, but torches that can defy the rain. They, range themselves in rows, they set off—it is the Belgian pilgrims having their last procession in Lourdes. I open the window, and now I can hear the singing too, the constantly repeated 'Avé, Avé, Avé, Maria!' In the grey dusk, in the pouring rain, the voices go on without ceasing, and a long time after I have closed the window I can still hear them, far away, like little bells ringing under water.

XIX

ZOLA AT LOURDES—THE MIRACLES IN HIS BOOK—
ELISE˜ ROUQUET, 'LA GRIVOTTE'—A FICTITIOUS
RELAPSE

CHARCOT and Bernheim have never visited Lourdes; their judgment on miracles is not based on personal investigation. But in the summer of 1892 a man who might justly be considered the delegate of modern France arrived at Lourdes; a man of letters, who had put experiment at the head of his programme, and who had made it his ambition to be the Claude Bernard of novel-writing. One day in August Émile Zola stepped out upon the platform at Lourdes.

Zola came well prepared. He had read the story of Bernadette and had conceived a sincere sympathy for 'the pure and upright personality of the seer, who was as far removed from lying and deceit as from pride and worldliness.' And now he retraced the footsteps of Bernadette everywhere in Lourdes, he even made a pilgrimage to Bartrès where she had at one time tended sheep; he took in impressions of the country, the town, the churches, the population, the pilgrims. In the Rue des Petits Fossés he trod reverently—the word is not too strong—across the threshold of the house in which the Soubirous had once lived, and into that one room which formed their whole apartment. ' It was a room ten to twelve feet square,' he says in his novel about Lourdes, ' with a stone floor and raftered ceiling, and two windows of different sizes overlooking a small yard, into which only a greenish, obscured light penetrated ; if you wanted to read in this room you would have to light a candle in the middle of the day. And in this confined space seven people had lived, the parents, two boys and three girls, without light, without air, almost without bread ; their existence must have been a living burial. Here was her room ; from this wretched place it had all come forth—here the child had slept in heavy dreams between her two little sisters ; from here she had stepped out on her life's journey. And no one came any more to this place, the manger was empty, was forgotten and forsaken, whilst the seed that she had sown grew up so abundantly out yonder in the grotto and gave to the world a miraculous harvest such as it had never before seen. The tears welled up in Pierre's eyes, and he murmured softly, " This is Bethlehem ! " '

Zola has a motive in this constant praise of Bernadette and the Abbé Peyramale ; it is that he may be able the more vehemently to attack the priests at the grotto and in the basilica. He brings the most serious accusations against them · of avarice and deceitfulness, and of having demoralised Lourdes, ' made a Sodom and Gomorrah of Bernadette's Bethlehem.' This latter side of the case seems to have been of great interest to Zola ; a coquettish shop-girl cannot speak in a subdued voice across the counter to a handsome young ecclesiastic without arousing the moral indignation of the author of ' Nana,' and making him scent improper relations. And the low-necked corsage and aggressive manners of a flower-girl -fire his apparently too inflammable imagination.

And yet Zola's book contains passages of great beauty. Read, for instance, in the nineteenth chapter, the magnificent description of the procession with Marie Guersaint, who has been cured, up the ascents to the basilica, and the Benediction from there over the sunny landscape. Here Zola is the poet who is carried away spontaneously, who sees, feels and describes.

But behind the poet stands the theorist Zola, the dogmatic naturalist, who has beforehand laid it down as a law that the supernatural does not exist, that a miracle is an impossibility, that whatever is so called is nervous excitement, auto-suggestion, something science can explain and label with its own proper name.

The heroine of the book, Marie Guersaint, is composed on the basis of this *parti pris*, and also her cure, foretold by the wise Parisian doctor. It is intended as a paradigma on Charcot's ' La Foi qui guérit.'

Starting from the same *parti pris*, Zola recomposes nearly all the *real* cures that he witnessed in Lourdes and that he wished to include in his book. He has justly been censured for this falsification of human documents.

Zola went to Lourdes in a pilgrim train ; already on the journey he wished to make the acquaintance of the sick, to see their sores, hear about their sufferings, in order to be able to judge better about their possible cures later. In the first chapters of his novel he gives a masterly description of the knowledge he obtained in this intimate way.

Amongst the invalids in Zola's train there was a young girl named Marie Lemarchand, in the novel she is called Elise Rouquet. She suffered from lupus in the face, and Zola gives the following description: ' Her scarf fell aside a little and Marie (Guersaint) shuddered. It was lupus, and it had spread little by little over the nose and mouth ; a rodent ulcer under the crust was still ravaging the mucous membrane. The face was elongated like a dog's nose, it looked repulsive, with bristling hair and big round eyes. The cartilage of the nose was almost consumed, the extremely swollen upper lip pulled the mouth up to one side like a crooked cleft, loathsome and shapeless. Blood and matter oozed out of the big, sallow ulcer.' [1] On the next page Zola shows us the patient eating. ' Elise Rouquet carefully put small pieces of bread into the gaping hole that formed her mouth. All the other passengers turned pale at this gruesome sight. And in the souls of all the same thought awoke: " Ah, dear blessed Virgin, all-merciful Mother of God, what a miracle if this can be cured ! " '

Zola saw this miracle accomplished.

He arrived at Lourdes on August 20, Marie Lemarchand therefore on the same day. On the following day Zola was present at the *Bureau des Constatations* when Marie Lemarchand came in. She was cured ! ' She exposed her face to view, as she took off her scarf. She said that since the morning she had washed her sores at the spring and that they were now beginning to heal up and grow paler. *This was actually true.*

[1] *Lourdes* (1903), p. 15.

Pierre (the hero of the book) saw that the face looked less repulsive.' [1]

Zola chooses his words carefully, but one perceives that he is confronted with something that has struck him with wonder and that he does not dare to deny. Yet Marie Lemarchand's case was really even more serious than as described by Zola. She suffered not only from lupus in both cheeks, in the eyelids, the lower part of the nose, the upper lip and the tongue—she also had lupus ulcers on other parts of her body, and both her lungs were attacked by tubercles. For three months she had had an incessant cough and had now and then expectorated blood.

Shortly before Marie Lemarchand came into the bureau, Zola had just happened to say to Dr. Boissarie that he wished he could see ' only so much as a cut finger come up whole from the baths.' [2] ' Here,' exclaimed the director of the medico-scientific bureau, ' here is what you are seeking, Monsieur Zola ; an ulcer visible to everyone and healed in a moment ! Just come and look carefully at this young girl.'

Zola laughed. ' I should like very much to look at her, but she must grow a little prettier first ! '

This wish, too, was granted him. Marie Lemarchand really did grow better-looking. The sceptical doctor in the novel, Dr. Ferrand, verifies this : ' It was now certain that the lupus that was devouring Elise Rouquet's face was improving. She continued her sponging treatment at the spring, and was just leaving the bureau where Dr. Bonnamy (i.e. Boissarie) was exulting about her. Ferrand went up to her, examined the sore which had already become paler and slightly dried up ; it was

---

[1] *Lourdes*, p. 194. Italics mine. [2] *Ibid.*, p. 193.

still far from being quite cured, but a process of healing was actively at work.' [1]

According to the account given in the ' Annales de Lourdes,' Marie Lemarchand's recovery was even more rapid than would appear from this description given by Zola. At that bath in the *piscinæ* she was cured, not only of the lupus from which she had been suffering, but also of tuberculosis. Her recovery was lasting ; sixteen years later, on November 7, 1908, she wrote to Dr. Boissarie : ' I am still perfectly well ; the terrible disease from which I suffered so much, and of which I was cured on August 21, 1892, has never again made its appearance. I was married six years ago, and now have five children. This will show you what a gift of grace I received at Lourdes ; from being a poor, miserable invalid I have become a strong, healthy woman and a happy mother. The Blessed Virgin does not do her work by halves.'

Zola wrote his novel the year after he had been in Lourdes. He ascribed the cure of Marie Lemarchand to auto-suggestion ; he considered her lupus to be ' an unknown formation of ulcers of hysterical origin.' It would have been interesting to know whether the great writer, with whom it was a point of honour to be a man of facts and an incorruptible witness to the truth, would have continued to believe in a suggestion that was powerful enough to endure in its effects after a period of sixteen years.

It is hardly possible that he would, for in his own novel, ' Lourdes,' he has shown that he does not ascribe such power to suggestion. In his book he has

[1] Tout un travail sourd de guérison commençait. *Lourdes*, pp. 363–364.

N

placed La Grivotte, whose cure he also witnessed at Lourdes, side by side with Elise Rouquet. This miracle too, he thought, was due to the nerves. After having described La Grivotte's recovery he therefore lets her have a relapse and die on the way home from Lourdes. This relapse, however, is *Zola's own fiction*, put into the book to support his theory.

The real name of La Grivotte was Marie Lebranchu. She was in the same pilgrim train as Elise Rouquet. Zola describes her in the following outlines: 'An emaciated face, wavy hair, and strangely brilliant eyes that made her almost beautiful. She was consumptive, and at a very advanced stage of the disease.'

Marie Lebranchu was cured on the same day as Marie Lemarchand. 'There was great excitement at this moment in the bureau—La Grivotte came rushing in like a whirlwind. "I am cured! I am cured!" She said that at first they had refused to bathe her and she had begged and implored and cried. She had a cold and was in a perspiration, but she had hardly been put into the icy water and been in three minutes before she felt her strength returning. It seemed as if there was a sudden flash of life right through her body. And now she was radiant, jumped and danced about, could not keep still. "I am cured! I am cured!"

' Pierre contemplated her. Was this the girl he had seen last night, lying on the seat in the railway carriage, coughing up blood, with a face the colour of clay? He did not recognise her as the same person as she stood there, erect, with rosy cheeks and sparkling eyes.' [1]

False excitement! Zola thought. A moment's

[1] *Lourdes*, p. 195.

rapture ! And in his book he lets her collapse again.

But Marie Lebranchu did *not* collapse. Next year she came back to Lourdes to have the permanency of her cure verified. In 1895 Zola himself looked her up in Paris, and was able to assure himself that she was not dead. Later on she married, became a widow, and she now lives as a servant in the house of some Sisters of Charity. Dr. Boissarie last heard from her in December, 1908, and her letter concludes : ' I shall probably never see you and Lourdes again, but I make a daily pilgrimage thither in my thoughts.'

There are only two explanations possible here. Either La Grivotte was never consumptive—but Zola's description quite coincides with Marie Le-branchu's medical certificate, with which he made himself acquainted at the bureau [1]—or else something happened that is beyond human understanding. Tuberculosis like that of Marie Lebranchu is not cured by suggestion, nor by cold baths.

Zola knew this, he therefore lets La Grivotte have a relapse and die. When Dr. Boissarie called on him one day in Paris, and asked him why he had made the story conclude in a way that was opposed to the actual facts, the famous novelist answered in a tone of annoyance, ' I suppose I am master of the persons in my own books and can let them live or die as I choose ? And besides,' he added, ' I don't believe in miracles. Even if *all* the sick in Lourdes were cured in one moment I would not believe in them ! '

---

[1] Her case is diagnosed as ' tuberculose pulmonaire avec ramollissement et cavernes.' The patient had been confined to bed for ten months and had lost 48 lbs. in weight. Boissarie, *L'Œuvre de Lourdes*, p. 323.

XX

THE USE OF MIRACLES—MIRACLE AND DOGMA— A LUTHERAN DEAN AT LOURDES

THOSE who have accompanied me so far as this will stop at these words of Zola, and they will ask me, ' What, then, is the use of all these miracles ? supposing that they *are* miracles.   When all is said and done it is the same as in the Gospels ; if they do not believe Moses and the prophets, neither will they believe though one should rise from the dead.'

This I quite admit.   Unbelief is not cured by miracles and doubt is endless.   In this respect Zola's attitude to the medical certificates placed before him at the *Bureau des Constatations* is typical.   ' Many of them were far too concise, others exceedingly clear and exhaustive.   Other certificates were furthermore provided with the signature of the local magistrate. Still one had a right to doubt.   Who was the doctor in question ?   Was he a competent member of his profession ?   Were his motives known ?   One felt tempted to institute inquiries with regard to each signature.'

Of course—how could it be otherwise ?   Outside the domain of the exact sciences it is altogether impossible to give an absolutely convincing proof

of anything at all. In all historical questions one
is dependent on the testimony available, and one
cannot arrive at a complete conviction of their credibility. One never gets further than probability, that
all *reasonable* doubt is excluded. But there is always
room for belief or unbelief.

Miracles, therefore, are not worked for the sake
of unbelievers, they are worked for those who believe.
In order to strengthen them, to confirm them in their
faith, to inspire them with ardour, and fill them with
new life and fervour. For how difficult it is, how
almost impossible, in the midst of our modern enlightenment, to keep hold of one's conviction of the existence
of the supernatural. Perhaps it is only an historical
illusion, but it seems to us that it would have been
easier to believe in God as the Almighty before man
himself became so mighty, easier to believe in God's
providence and God's paternal love before the vault of
heaven's roof was shattered to pieces, and we, from
our corner of the universe, gazed terror-stricken into
a cosmic infinity where there is no longer any Jacob's
ladder with angels ascending and descending, but only
the relentless forces of nature moving onwards at a
whirling speed in their eternal orbits.

Ah, how hard it is, in view of the doctrine of
modern psychology and physiology about the relations
between soul and body, about the simultaneous
decay, dissolution and disappearance of both—how
hard it is to keep hold of the old, simple creed : I
believe in the resurrection of the body ; I believe in
the life everlasting. Where are they now, all those
who have said this through the ages ? Moulded away
in their graves, become earth in earth, dust in dust ;

And shall it ever be sounded, that *novissima tuba*, that rousing trumpet that Saint Paul hoped for, at whose voice all shall rise from their graves—as on the naïve altar-piece by Fra Angelico ? Saint Paul and all the apostles are dead. Is it not an everlasting death ? Mary, the Mother of Jesus, died. And is not her assumption into heaven a mere legend—only a beautiful picture on a background of gold ? And Jesus Himself, He died too. And did He ever rise again ? The disciples saw the empty tomb. But was Mary Magdalene not instinctively right when she asked, ' Where have they laid Him ? ' They had laid Him in another place—they, Joseph of Arimathæa and Nicodemus,—that was the whole miracle of the Resurrection !

In view of such doubts, God must come to the assistance of His faithful. A Lutheran minister of the Danish National Church has given an impressive account of his spiritual anguish during the assaults of such thoughts as these, and has described how he fought his way through them. But that method is possible only for the few, for those who have knowledge and time and—not least—means to give up a year or two of their lives to investigate to its very roots the question about which the contention goes on. As surely as Christianity is not the concern of the learned only, there must be another weapon against doubt.

This weapon is the miraculous, and it is a weapon in two ways. First, because it is the evidence of a power that is higher than Nature and that answers our prayers, gives us what we ask for. Such a power as this is what all ages and all nations, from Hellas to the Fiji Islands, have understood by the term God.

.

But, secondly, the miraculous is closely related to dogma. Christian doctrines, for instance, about the Trinity, about the Virgin Birth of Jesus, His Resurrection, His Ascension, are rejected by many because they are unthinkable. This is true, they *are* unthinkable. We can accept these sentences as correct, i.e. corresponding to actual facts, but we cannot connect them with any concrete idea in our minds.

The same peculiarity, however, holds good of the miraculous. It can be verified, but it cannot be imagined. All processes of healing known to us are consecutive, dependent on time, consist of a series of changes linked together by advancements from one stage to another. At Lourdes the recoveries occur suddenly, instantaneously, accomplishing in a few hours or days that which it would otherwise take months or years to achieve. And the connection between cause and effect is cancelled to such an extent that the same water, used as a bath or a lotion, now fills up a pair of hollow lungs, now heals up caries or cures an abdominal inflammation. Either the water at Lourdes contains wonderful, hitherto unknown properties—but then, why are these properties not always and regularly effective according to a law that ought to be discoverable ?—or else it is God that works here, the God of Abraham, Isaac and Jacob, the God of the prophets, the God of Jesus, the God of the Apostles, He who kindled the wood of Elijah's pile on Mount Carmel with fire from Heaven, and healed the sick in Jerusalem by means of Peter's shadow.

This line of thought is not very modern, and perhaps it will be least acceptable to the theologians of the present day. However this may be, I remember having read in a handbook on the philosophy of religion, written by a Lutheran minister, a licentiate in theology, that 'we are unacquainted with miracles at the present day; they do not occur within the experience of modern humanity. The accounts given by the Catholic Church of miracles are of such a nature that it is best to ignore them.' And another influential Danish theologian has quite cursorily and contemptuously spoken of those 'who still, in our age, boast of authenticated miracles.'

The truth is that the impossibility of the miraculous, or—what comes to the same thing—the impossibility of verifying the miraculous—is a fundamental dogma in the modern outlook of the world. Such dogmas, however, have this in common with so many other modern productions, that they look more formidable than they are. They are not so well reasoned out as they would seem to be, perhaps that is why they are enunciated with so much the more assurance and with an air of assuming that the last word on this matter has been said long ago. I have long had my suspicions about this scientific high-and-mightiness that declines even to enter on any discussion, not to mention investigation of facts, which might endanger its system. And in order to justify these suspicions of mine, I would mention that about a little more than a century ago it was still a settled question amongst men of science in Europe that meteor stones could not be of cosmic origin, that they did not come to us from space outside. The learned Professor Stütz of Vienna, in speaking of a large meteor stone that had fallen at Agram in 1751, simply wrote, in 1790, that 'it may perhaps have been believed, even by the most enlightened minds in Germany in 1751, when great ignorance still prevailed with regard to natural history and physics, that iron could drop down from the sky. In our own day it would be unpardonable to find such fairy tales even probable.' In several museums meteor stones were even thrown away, as it was not desirable to be considered foolish for having kept them! At about the same time, however, as the publication of Stütz's article, that is in 1790, a meteor stone took the liberty of falling down near Juillac in France, and the mayor of the town then sent a report of the fall, signed by three hundred eye-witnesses, to the Academy of Sciences in Paris. And behold! this appeal to the highest scientific authority in the country was not made in vain! Bertholon placed the report before the members of the Academy with sincere regrets 'that not only the mayor of the town, but its entire population, by an official statement, testifies to a popular legend that one can only contemplate with pity. What am I to do with such a document? The philosophically cultured reader will at once form his own opinion when he peruses this authentic testimony to an evidently false fact, a physically impossible phenomenon!'

If I am not quite mistaken, then, in this matter, I see science of 1790 with an air of sternness and a consciousness of her outraged dignity firmly and gravely rejecting those who ' boast of authenticated falls of meteor stones.' Meteor stones might fall as thick as hail and be as large as ostrich eggs—science knows better; they *cannot* fall, therefore they *do not* fall! The old scholastics taught that when anything was real it was always possible—*ab esse ad posse valet consequentia.* Modern science has turned the sentence round ; when anything, in her opinion, is impossible, she gives it her marching orders to depart out of reality. In more unenlightened times people believe what they saw. But ' in our times ' we are too wise to do that. ' If I saw such a stone fall down to my feet,' said the learned Deluc, after Bertholon had spoken, ' I should, of course, have to say that I had seen it, yet I should not be able to believe it.' ' It is better,' Vaudin declared, ' simply to deny such incredible things than to attempt any explanation.'

Thus spoke science ' of the present day ' in 1790 ; thus she still speaks in 1910. Let fire fall down from heaven, or let the sick be made whole at Lourdes as in a new pool of Bethsaida, still the answer is the same self-assured, imperturbable, ' It is impossible, it does not happen.' ' Science of the present day' is always true to herself, in the eighteenth as in the twentieth century.

This book, therefore, is not written *for* her, it is written against her.

After all, I am not alone, there are others on my side. It is true they are not great theologians, whose works are able to command, alas, only a conditional and very condescending, but oh ! so valuable an acknowledgment from free-thinking philosophers. But, for instance, a worthy old Danish village pastor, the late Dean Aleth Hansen, who in his time also visited Lourdes, and who described his travels in a little book called ' From Arcachon to Nîmes,' published in 1892, very quietly and without making any stir.

Aleth Hansen did not deny the reality of the

miracles that happen at Lourdes. He has the same conception of them as of the cures by means of prayer and laying on of hands which have often been performed by believing Lutheran Christians, in reliance on the words in the Epistle of St. James v. 14–17, by Zeller of Männedorf, by Blumhardt of Bol (Württemberg). Aleth Hansen writes that 'these communities at Bol and Männedorf have awakened to a full consciousness that signs and wonders must occur in the Church, as they did of old in the days of the Apostles, if the Church is indeed built on the foundations laid down by the Apostles and Prophets, with Jesus Christ as the chief corner-stone.'

With regard to Lourdes, the Danish ecclesiastic says that here Mary is invoked 'as the loving Mother, to whom petitions are made to lead souls suffering from sin and disease to the Saviour, and also to make intercession for their temporal and eternal salvation with Him.' And it seems to me that a petition for such help and support from the Virgin Mary is—so far as I can see—from a Christian standpoint quite reasonable and warrantable. Further, as the sick and suffering are required to confess their transgressions, it can quite well be reconciled with the 'prayer of the righteous' in Männedorf and Bol, in the way inculcated at Jerusalem. The Church, this quite unmodern author says in conclusion, 'is more than a mere name and a mere nominal value, it is a living reality and a community endowed with vital power, and thanks be to the living Lord of the Church, Who is personally with His own " all days until the consummation of the world," there are movements in the Church of deep, wonderful, and wonder-working forces.'

XXI

THROUGH MARY TO JESUS—THE SPIRITUAL MIRACLES—
ON THE MONT DES BRETONS

IT is my last day in Lourdes—the eighth day since my arrival.

The Belgians have left ; early this morning I saw Augusta de Muynck and Julia Witthamer, the two inseparable friends, kneeling together at the grotto ; they were paying their farewell visit to Our Lady. The Bretons, too, are gone, the space round the baths is almost deserted. Only the Basques remain ; from the *Bureau des Constatations*, where I have called to say good-bye, I can hear them singing in the Rosary Church. The deep metallic voices are ringing out ; listen, it is the Credo : ' et in Jesum Christum, Filium Dei unigenitum, et ex Patre natum ante omnia sæcula, Deum de Deo, lumen de lumine, Deum verum de Deo vero,'—and in Jesus Christ, the only-begotten Son of God, begotten of the Father before all worlds, God of God, Light of Light, true God of true God—

' Yes,' says Dr. Boissarie, who has been listening too for a moment ; ' that is the greatest and the real significance of Lourdes, " Per Mariam ad Jesum "— the white Virgin of Massabieille would fain bring all these multitudes to her son.'

And the old doctor begins to speak of the religious significance of Lourdes. He mentions the number of communicants; on an average about half a million communions are given yearly, and last year, the jubilee year of 1908, this number rose to even nearly seven hundred thousand.

'Huysmans was right,' he continues, 'when it seemed to him that in Lourdes he was moved back to the ages of faith; as it was in the Middle Ages there are now whole companies of pilgrims who, during their stay, have no other abode than the Church. It is their house, their hotel. In the evening the Blessed Sacrament is exposed on the High Altar and the pilgrims spend the night in prayer before it. . . . Then in the earliest hours of the morning the priests begin to say Mass, sometimes an altar is set up on the platform outside the Church and Mass is then said in the open air, under a sky luminous with stars. It is hardly possible to imagine anything more impressive, more solemn. I was present one night when Monsignor Gieure said Pontifical Mass in the open air, and whilst Mass was being said *twelve* priests went on unceasingly giving Holy Communion. This constant stream of communicants lasted *two hours.*

'And this is by no means a unique instance. I remember another time, inside the Rosaire—the pilgrims from Les Landes were here—five thousand of these worthy people spent the night in prayer in the church, and the Communion in the morning lasted three whole hours. There were between two and three thousand who went to Communion.

'Yes,' the old doctor continues, 'God does mighty works in Lourdes—the cures are not the greatest miracles—no, all the conversions that occur—they are not all saints, those that come here.   Many come out of consideration for others, or take it as an opportunity for a change and make a holiday of their visit here.   Add to these the numerous tourists who come out of curiosity, or as doubters, as sceptics, as mockers. . . .

‘ Ah, if the confessionals in the crypt of the basilica and in the Rosaire could speak—if the lips of the confessors were not sealed !   But it is of course impossible to set up any *bureau des constatations* on that side of the matter.   Nevertheless, the priests cannot refrain, from time to time, from expressing their happiness, their astonishment, at the wonderful conversions that they are permitted to witness here.   Often the penitents themselves, for the glory of God and our Blessed Lady, speak of the grace that has been conferred on them in Lourdes.   These things always leak out, and we can judge from them that Lourdes is, above all, the promised land of grace, a fountain of healing for diseased consciences, a gigantic sanatorium for souls.

‘ And indeed the Blessed Virgin did make it known that this was her object when she bade Bernadette proclaim repentance.   Penance, Penance :   those words from the lips of Our Lady are assuredly the profoundest explanation why Lourdes exists. . . .

‘ Notice, too, how Mary, as it were, retires, takes a second place in the cures that occur.   Every year fewer and fewer are cured at the grotto and in the baths, more and more at the Benediction of the Blessed Sacrament.   At first the eucharistic cures were only a fifth or a sixth of the entire number, now they amount to one half or more.   One of the most beautiful cures we have had this year, on February 11 last, happened at the moment when the invalid received Holy Communion. It was Mademoiselle Philiberte Dionet, who had suffered for eighteen months from spinal tuberculosis, from Pott's disease, and who was cured in one instant.

' It has always been Mary's highest wish to bring mankind to her Son. . . . " Whatsoever He tells you, that do ye," she says in the Gospel and leads those who ask for help to Him. Here in Lourdes, too, she seeks gradually to step into the background, more and more to give all the glory to Our Lord. She has prepared the way ; now it is He Who is to make His triumphal entry. *Per Mariam ad Jesum—* in these words of Saint Bernard the aim of Lourdes is expressed as in a formula : Through Mary to Jesus ! '

We are alone in the bureau, Dr. Boissarie and I ; at my request he gives me some information on one or two more points. Then visitors begin to arrive, not any sick who are cured, but other pilgrims, a few ecclesiastics, a couple of foreign doctors. Soon the old doctor has a whole circle around him.

I stand for a few minutes contemplating the photographs in large frames on the walls, of invalids who have been cured. I see Madame Rouchel, the lupus patient from Metz, a *pendant* to Zola's Elise Rouquet. Marie Borel, with the terrible abdominal ulcers, cured after one bath in the *piscinæ* ; ' the two skeletons,' as Dr. Boissarie generally calls them, two dreadfully emaciated young women, looking, on their photographs before their cure, like nothing but two frameworks of bones, and a year later like two radiantly healthy young girls. . . .

Then I turn to say good-bye to Dr. Boissarie. He stretches out his hand to me in an abstracted manner.

' See you to-morrow, then ? '

' No, doctor ; I am going away.'

' Oh, you are going away, yes, of course. *Eh, bien !* ' And the old doctor comes close to me, embraces me cordially, and we kiss each other on both cheeks.

An hour later I sit on the top of the Mont des Bretons, so called because the Breton pilgrims have made a road with the fourteen Stations of the Cross up its sides and set up an enormous crucifix on the summit. It is the highest point of the Espélugues hill and towers far above the spire of the basilica.

On the way up I passed the hideous groups of gaudily coloured statues forming the stations, and I understand the rage of Huysmans against these artistic (or rather inartistic) horrors. And yet— and yet—all this about art becomes a matter of such indifference at Lourdes, it seems to me, and one would need to be a more hardened æsthetic than I am, to be able to waste one's indignation on the lack of taste that one encounters here and there. The fact is, Catholic art is dead and will never again rise from the grave. Besides, there are *other* wonders that are more necessary.

And if art, or rather, the manufacture of religious statues, sins at Lourdes, Nature makes ample compensation. How wonderful, for instance, is the river Gave ! Last night I was again at the grotto. After the rainy day the evening was clear and cool. The last clouds rose up like white smoke amongst the mountains before the pale gold of the evening sky.

And the river foamed and rushed onwards between its green banks, reflecting at first the pallid blue of the sky, later, when it grew darker, silvery blue, wonderfully alive, with light bluish-white vapours against the sombre trees.

And now I am sitting here on the top of the Mont des Bretons, where three great bare crosses have been set up in a mound of stones. Down the sides the mountain is clothed with trees, but on the level at the summit there is only grass, sprinkled here and there with white clover. Quite small fir trees, sycamores and rowan, all newly planted, are dotted round about ; large grey boulders and slabs lie spread here and there. I sit on the southern slope of the hill and look down into the upper valley of the Gave. On either side other mountains rise up, covered near the base with the dark green of trees, higher up with the brighter hue of pastures ; furthest away fading into a chilly blue with patches and grooves of snow on the peaked ridges beneath an unsettled and cloudy sky. I hear the roaring of the river in the depths below and the muffled sound of a cow bell from a slope that I cannot see. The grey clouds lower, drooping with heavy ragged edges over the distant snow peaks. For a moment they scatter and a shred of sky peeps out ; there is an angelic softness in its faint and pallid blue. But soon everything is again dark and gloomy, some big drops of rain begin to fall, the tall grass rustles about me in the cold wind.

Here I bid farewell to the country of Bernadette.

XXII

TAKING LEAVE OF LOURDES—HOMEWARDS

In the evening I pay a last visit to the grotto. The rain is pouring, as on most of the preceding evenings, and I splash through shallow lakes ; the pilgrims have had to give up the torch-light procession and have taken refuge in the immense hall of the Rosary. A brilliant light streams out from the open doors and shines on the glistening pavement ; they are singing within.

There is no one at the grotto, but there it is, low and bright, shining out on the wet, dark night—a place of refuge and light in the midst of a world of darkness.

Next morning the train bears me away from Lourdes. I travel towards Biarritz ; the railway line runs along the banks of the Gave, and a little way outside the town Massabieille can be seen on the other side of the river. I send a last farewell across, catch a glimpse of the white statue, see a number of people gathered before it—new pilgrims must have arrived this morning. . . . Then the vision is gone ; I can still see the basilica in the background, and the old fortress, lonely and towering—and Le Grand Ger, with its cross on the top—and furthest away the gleaming snow peaks. . . . Still a few moments and all has vanished. The line bends, only the Gave flows faithfully on.

My journey first goes westwards—then to the north, further and further north. . . . To the old, Gothic Bayonne and the Atlantic at Biarritz—then *via* Bordeaux to Paris, and from Paris homewards in long day's marches : Paris—Cologne ; Cologne—Hamburg ; Hamburg—Kiel ; Kiel—Korsör—Copenhagen, a long journey with two so different extremities : the grotto of Our Lady of Lourdes, with the sick at the miraculous fountain, and the square of the Town Hall in the capital of Denmark, with young people in gay summer attire round the café tables in front of the Hotel Bristol. . . .

From my long journey I have brought home two things—a bottle of Lourdes water which friends in the north have asked me to bring—and the rough draft of a book.

The bottle of water from the spring has long since reached its destination ; it was received gratefully As for the book, it is now written, and it goes forth into a world that I know has not asked for it.

THE END

PRINTED BY
SPOTTISWOODE AND CO. LTD., COLCHESTER
LONDON AND ETON

A CLASSIFIED LIST OF WORKS

BY

ROMAN CATHOLIC WRITERS

TABLE OF CONTENTS

LONGMANS, GREEN & CO.

39 PATERNOSTER ROW, LONDON, E.C.

FOURTH AVENUE AND THIRTIETH STREET, NEW YORK
323 EAST TWENTY-THIRD STREET, CHICAGO
8 HORNBY ROAD, BOMBAY
303 BOWBAZAR STREET, CALCUTTA

1914

Stonyhurst Philosophical Series.

Edited by the Rev. RICHARD F. CLARKE, S.J.

Crown 8vo.

Extract from a Letter of His Holiness the Pope to the Bishop of Salford, on the Philosophical Course at Stonyhurst.

"You will easily understand, Venerable Brother, the pleasure We felt in what you reported to Us about the College of Stonyhurst in your diocese, namely, that by the efforts of the Superiors of this College, an excellent course of the exact sciences has been successfully set on foot, by establishing professorships, and by publishing in the vernacular for their students text-books of Philosophy, following the Principles of St. Thomas Aquinas. On this work We earnestly congratulate the Superiors and teachers of the College, and by letter We wish affectionately to express Our good-will towards them."

LOGIC.   By the Rev. RICHARD F. CLARKE, S.J.   5s.

FIRST PRINCIPLES OF KNOWLEDGE.   By the Rev. JOHN RICKABY, S.J.   5s.

MORAL PHILOSOPHY (Ethics and Natural Law).   By the Rev. JOSEPH RICKABY, S.J., M.A.   5s.

NATURAL THEOLOGY.   By the Rev. BERNARD BOEDDER, S.J.   6s. 6d.

PSYCHOLOGY, EMPIRICAL AND RATIONAL.   By the Rev. MICHAEL MAHER, S.J., D.Litt., M.A.   6s. 6d.

GENERAL METAPHYSICS.   By the Rev. JOHN RICKABY, S.J.   5s.

POLITICAL ECONOMY.   By CHAS. S. DEVAS, M.A.   7s. 6d.

THEORIES OF KNOWLEDGE: Absolutism, Pragmatism, Realism.   By LESLIE J. WALKER, S.J., M.A.   9s.

The Westminster Version of the Sacred Scriptures.

Undertaken with the approval of the Cardinal Archbishop and the Catholic Hierarchy.

Newly Translated from the Original Text. With Introduction, Critical and Explanatory Notes, Appendices, and Maps.

General Editors: The Rev. CUTHBERT LATTEY, S.J., Professor of Sacred Scripture at St. Beuno's College, North Wales, and the Rev. JOSEPH KEATING, S.J., Editor of *The Month.*

The collaboration, as Editors of separate Sections, of the Right Rev. Dr. McINTYRE, Bishop of Lamus; the Right Rev. Mgr. B. WARD, President of St. Edmund's; the Rev. J. P. ARENDZEN, Professor of Sacred Scripture at St. Edmund's; Father HUGH POPE, O.P., of the Collegio Angelico, Rome; Father JOSEPH RICKABY, S.J., of Oxford, and many other leading Catholic Scripture scholars, has been secured.

THE NEW TESTAMENT.

Vol. I.   ST. MATTHEW, ST. MARK, ST. LUKE. *In preparation.*

Vol. II.   ST. JOHN, THE ACTS OF THE APOSTLES. *In preparation.*

Vol. III.   ST. PAUL'S EPISTLES TO THE CHURCHES.

Part I.   THE EPISTLES TO THE THESSALONIANS. By the Rev. CUTHBERT LATTEY, S.J. 8vo. Paper covers, 6d. *net;* half cloth boards, 1s. *net.*

Part II.   THE FIRST EPISTLE TO THE CORINTHIANS. *In the press.*

Vol. IV.   THE OTHER CANONICAL EPISTLES. THE

The Westminster Library.

A Series of Manuals for Catholic Priests and Students.

Edited by the Right Rev. Monsignor BERNARD WARD, President of St. Edmund's College, and the Rev. HERBERT THURSTON, S.J.

Crown 8vo.

THE HOLY EUCHARIST. By the Right Rev. JOHN CUTHBERT HEDLEY, O.S.B., Bishop of Newport. 3s. 6d. *net.*

THE MASS: a Study of the Roman Liturgy. By the Rev. ADRIAN FORTESCUE, Ph.D., D.D. 6s. *net.*

THE NEW PSALTER AND ITS USE. By the Rev. E. H. BURTON, D.D., Vice-President of St. Edmund's College, Ware, and the Rev. EDWARD MYERS, M.A. 3s. 6d. *net.*

THE PRIEST'S STUDIES. By the Very Rev. THOMAS SCANNELL, D.D., Canon of Southwark Cathedral, Editor of *The Catholic Dictionary.* 3s. 6d. *net.*

THE TRADITION OF SCRIPTURE: its Origin, Authority and Interpretation. By the Very Rev. WILLIAM BARRY, D.D., Canon of Birmingham. 3s. 6d. *net.*

THE LEGENDS OF THE SAINTS: An Introduction to Hagiography. From the French of Père H. DELEHAYE, S.J., Bollandist. Translated by Mrs. V. M. CRAWFORD. 3s. 6d. *net.*

NON-CATHOLIC DENOMINATIONS. By the Very Rev. Monsignor ROBERT HUGH BENSON. 3s. 6d. *net.*

The following Volumes are in Preparation :—

THE EARLY CHURCH IN THE LIGHT OF THE MONUMENTS. By the Right Rev. Monsignor A. S. BARNES, M.A. With Illustrations. 5s. *net.*

THE CLERGY AND SOCIAL ACTION. By the Rev. CHARLES PLATER, S.J.

THE INSTRUCTION OF CONVERTS. By the Rev. SYDNEY F. SMITH, S.J.

For the Clergy and Students.

PRIMITIVE CATHOLICISM: By Monsignor PIERRE
BATIFFOL. Authorised translation by HENRY L. BRIANCEAU,
St. Mary's Seminary, Baltimore, revised by the Author. 8vo. 12s. 6d. *net.*

THE CREDIBILITY OF THE GOSPEL. "Orpheus
et l'Évangile." By Monsignor PIERRE BATIFFOL. Translated by the
Rev. G. C. H. POLLEN, S.J. With an Appendix giving the Decisions
of the Pontifical Biblical Commission, June 19th, 1911, and June 26th, 1912.
Crown 8vo. 4s. 6d. *net.*

    ** The Appendix will be supplied separately on application to the Publishers.

HISTORY OF THE ROMAN BREVIARY. By
Monsignor PIERRE BATIFFOL. Translated from the Third French
Edition, by the Rev. A. M. Y. BAYLAY, M.A. With a New Chapter
on the Decree of Pius X. 8vo. 9s. *net.*

HANDBOOK OF THE HISTORY OF PHILOSOPHY.
By Dr. ALBERT STÖCKL. Translated by the Rev. T. A. FINLAY,
S.J., M.A., National University, Dublin. 2 vols. 8vo.
Vol. I. PRE-SCHOLASTIC AND SCHOLASTIC PHILOSOPHY.
10s. 6d. *net.*
Vol. II. *In preparation.*

SCHOLASTICISM, Old and New: an Introduction to
Scholastic Philosophy, Mediæval and Modern. By MAURICE DE
WULF, Professor at the University of Louvain. Translated by P. COFFEY,
Ph.D. (Louvain), Professor of Logic and Metaphysics, Maynooth College,
Ireland. 8vo. 6s. *net.*

HISTORY OF MEDIEVAL PHILOSOPHY. By
MAURICE D. WULF. Translated by P. COFFEY, Ph.D. 8vo.
10s. 6d. *net.*

THE SCIENCE OF LOGIC: an Inquiry into the Principles
of Accurate Thought and Scientific Method. By P. COFFEY, Ph.D.
(Louvain), Professor of Logic and Metaphysics, Maynooth College, Ireland.
2 vols. 8vo.
Vol. I. Conception, Judgment, and Inference. 7s. 6d. *net.*
Vol. II. Method, Science, and Certitude. 7s. 6d. *net.*

MOTIVE-FORCE AND MOTIVATION-TRACKS:
a Research in Will Psychology. By E. BOYD BARRETT, S.J., Doctor
of Philosophy, Superior Institute, Louvain, M.A., Honours Graduate
National University, Ireland. 8vo, 7s. 6d. *net;* paper covers, 6s. *net.*

OUTLINES OF DOGMATIC THEOLOGY. By
SYLVESTER JOSEPH HUNTER, S.J. Crown 8vo. Three vols.
6s. 6d. each.

STUDIES ON THE GOSPELS. By VINCENT ROSE,
O.P., Professor in the University of Fribourg. Translated by ROBERT
FRASER, D.D., Domestic Prelate to H.H. Pius X. Crown 8vo. 6s. *net.*

For the Clergy and Students—*continued.*

THEODICY : Essays on Divine Providence. By ANTONIO
ROSMINI SERBATI. Translated with some Omissions from the Italian
Edition of 1845. 3 vols. Crown 8vo. 21s. *net.*

THOUGHTS OF A CATHOLIC ANATOMIST. By
THOMAS DWIGHT, M.D., LL.D., Parkman Professor of Anatomy
at Harvard. Crown 8vo. 3s. 6d. *net.*

ESSAYS IN PASTORAL MEDICINE. By AUSTIN
O'MALLEY, M.D., Ph.D., LL.D., Pathologist and Ophthalmologist to
Saint Agnes's Hospital, Philadelphia ; and JAMES J. WALSH, Ph.D.,
LL.D., Adjunct Professor of Medicine at the New York Polytechnic
School for Graduates in Medicine. 8vo. 10s. 6d. *net.*

* *The term ' Pastoral Medicine " may be said to represent that part of medicine which
is of import to a pastor in his cure, and those divisions of ethics and moral theology which
concern a physician in his practice. This book is primarily intended for Roman Catholic
confessors.*

BODILY HEALTH AND SPIRITUAL VIGOUR. A
Book for Preachers and Teachers. By WILLIAM J. LOCKINGTON,
S.J. With Illustrations. Crown 8vo. 2s. 6d. *net.*

THE SCIENCE OF ETHICS. By Rev. MICHAEL
CRONIN, M.A., D.D., Ex-Fellow, Royal University of Ireland ;
Professor, Clonliffe College, Dublin. 8vo.

Vol. I., General Ethics. 12s. 6d. *net.*

THE OLD RIDDLE AND THE NEWEST ANSWER.
An Enquiry how far Modern Science has altered the aspect of the Problem
of the Universe. By JOHN GERARD, S.J., F.L.S. Crown 8vo.
2s. 6d. *net.* Popular Edition. Paper Covers. 6d.

* *An examination of the assumptions of Haeckel's " The Riddle of the Universe".*

THE KEY TO THE WORLD'S PROGRESS : an
Essay on Historical Logic, being some Account of the Historical Significance
of the Catholic Church. By CHARLES STANTON DEVAS, M.A.
Crown 8vo. 5s. *net.* Popular Edition. Paper covers, 6d.

* *The object of this book is to give to the logic and history of Newman an economic or
sociological setting, and thus to show that " for the explanation of World-history we must
first have the true theory of the Christian Church and her life through eighteen centuries".
Part I. states briefly the problems which the philosophy of history seeks to resolve. Part II.
presents the solution offered by Christianity and takes the form of an historical analysis of the
principles by which the Church has been guided in her relations with the world.*

For the Clergy and Students—*continued.*

THE PRICE OF UNITY. By the Rev. B. W. MATURIN.
Crown 8vo. 5s. *net.*

THE CATHOLIC CHURCH FROM WITHIN. With
a Preface by His Eminence CARDINAL VAUGHAN, formerly
Archbishop of Westminster. Crown 8vo. 6s. 6d. *net.*

CARDINAL NEWMAN AND THE ENCYCLICAL
PASCENDI DOMINICI GREGIS. An Essay by the Most Rev.
EDWARD THOMAS O'DWYER, Bishop of Limerick. 8vo.
Paper Covers, 1s. *net.*

BISHOP GORE AND THE CATHOLIC CLAIMS.
By Dom JOHN CHAPMAN, O.S.B. 8vo. Paper Covers, 6d. *net* ;
cloth, 1s. *net.*

ASPECTS OF ANGLICANISM; or, Some Comments
on Certain Incidents in the 'Nineties. By Mgr. JAMES MOYES, D.D.,
Canon of Westminster Cathedral. Crown 8vo. 2s. 6d. *net.* Paper Covers,
2s. *net.*

LENT AND HOLY WEEK: Chapters on Catholic Ob-
servance and Ritual. By the Rev. HERBERT THURSTON, S.J.
Crown 8vo. 6s. *net.*

SOME PAPERS OF LORD ARUNDELL OF WAR-
DOUR, 12th BARON, COUNT OF THE HOLY ROMAN
EMPIRE, Etc. With a Preface by the Dowager LADY ARUN-
DELL OF WARDOUR. With Portrait. 8vo. 8s. 6d. *net.*

*A memorial volume consisting of a collection of Lord Arundell's writings, the thoughts
that he wrote down after reading, or which were intended to be spoken in Parliament, to his
tenantry, or at public meetings. The contents of the volume are divided as follows : Social
Inequality and Natural Right—Home Politics—Pope and Queen—Foreign Politics—The
Nature Myth Theory.*

PSYCHOLOGY OF POLITICS AND HISTORY. By
the Rev. J. A. DEWE, M.A. Crown 8vo. 5s. *net.*

THE REAL DEMOCRACY (First Essays of the Rota
Club). By J. E. F. MANN, N. J. SIEVERS, and R. W. T. COX.
Crown 8vo. 4s. 6d. *net.*

*These essays are a defence of the principle of Property as a determining factor in the
economic and political structure of the State.*

THE MONTH; A Catholic Magazine. Conducted by
FATHERS OF THE SOCIETY OF JESUS. Published Monthly.
8vo. Paper Covers, 1s. ; Covers for binding volumes, 1s. *net.*

INDEX TO THE MONTH, 1864-1908. Arranged
under Subjects and Authors. 8vo. Cloth. 3s. 6d. *net.* Interleaved with
Writing Paper. 5s. *net.*

STONYHURST PHILOSOPHICAL SERIES.
For particulars see page 2.

History.

THE LIFE AND TIMES OF BISHOP CHALLONER,
1691-1781. By EDWIN H. BURTON, D.D., F.R.Hist.S., Vice-President of St. Edmund's College, Ware. With 34 Portraits and other Illustrations. 2 vols. 8vo. 25s. *net.*

THE DAWN OF THE CATHOLIC REVIVAL IN
ENGLAND, 1781-1803. By the Right Rev. Monsignor BERNARD WARD, F.R.Hist.S., President of St. Edmund's College, Ware. With 38 Illustrations. 2 vols. 8vo. 25s. *net.*

THE EVE OF CATHOLIC EMANCIPATION.
Being the History of the English Catholics during the first Thirty Years of the Nineteenth Century. By the Right Rev. Monsignor BERNARD WARD, F.R.Hist.S. With Portraits and other Illustrations. 3 vols. 8vo.

Vols. I. and II.—1803-1820. 21s. *net.*

Vol. III.—1820-1829. 12s. 6d. *net.*

THE DOMINICAN REVIVAL IN THE NINE-
TEENTH CENTURY. Being some Account of the Restoration of the Order of Preachers throughout the World under Father Jandel, the seventy-third Master-General. By Father RAYMUND DEVAS, O.P. With Portraits. Crown 8vo. 3s. 6d. *net.*

BEGINNINGS, OR GLIMPSES OF VANISHED
CIVILIZATIONS. By MARION M'MURROUGH MULHALL, Member of the Roman Arcadia. Crown 8vo. 2s. 6d. *net.*

History—*continued*.

THE STORY OF ANCIENT IRISH CIVILISATION.
By P. W. JOYCE, LL.D., M.R.I.A. Fcp. 8vo. 1s. 6d. *net.*

A SMALLER SOCIAL HISTORY OF ANCIENT
IRELAND. By P. W. JOYCE, LL.D., M.R.I.A. With 13 Illustrations. Crown 8vo. 3s. 6d. *net.*

A SHORT HISTORY OF IRELAND, from the Earliest
Times to 1608. By P. W. JOYCE, LL.D., M.R.I.A. With Map. Crown 8vo. 10s. 6d.

THE ORIGIN AND HISTORY OF IRISH NAMES
OF PLACES. By P. W. JOYCE, LL.D., M.R.I.A. 3 vols. Crown 8vo. 5s. each.

THE WONDERS OF IRELAND; and other Papers on
Irish Subjects. By P. W. JOYCE, LL.D., M.R.I.A. Crown 8vo. 2s. 6d. *net.*

STOLEN WATERS: a Page from the Conquest of Ulster.
By T. M. HEALY, K.C., M.P., Bencher of King's Inns, Dublin, and of Gray's Inn, London. 8vo. 10s. 6d. *net.*

HISTORY OF THE SOCIETY OF JESUS IN NORTH
AMERICA: Colonial and Federal. By THOMAS HUGHES of the same Society. Royal 8vo.

TEXT.

Volume I. From the First Colonization, 1580, till 1645. With 3 Maps and 3 Facsimiles. 15s. *net.*

Volume II. *In preparation.*

Volume III. *In preparation.*

DOCUMENTS.

Volume I. Part I. Nos. 1-140 (1605-1838). With 2 Maps and 5 Facsimiles. 21s. *net.*

Volume I. Part II. Nos. 141-224 (1605-1838). With 3 Facsimiles. 21s. *net.*

Works by the Author of " The Life of a Prig," etc.

POLICY AND PAINT; or Some Incidents in the Lives of Dudley Carleton and Peter Paul Rubens. With 14 Illustrations. 8vo. 9s. *net.*

VICES IN VIRTUES AND OTHER VAGARIES. 8vo. 3s. 6d. *net.*

THE FIRST DUKE AND DUCHESS OF NEW-CASTLE-UPON-TYNE.   With Portrait and 15 other Illustrations. 8vo. 10s. 6d. *net.*

THE CURIOUS CASE OF LADY PURBECK : A Scandal of the Seventeenth Century. 8vo. 6s. *net.*

PRYINGS AMONG PRIVATE PAPERS : Chiefly of the Seventeenth and Eighteenth Centuries. 8vo. 7s. 6d. *net.*

ROCHESTER AND OTHER LITERARY RAKES OF THE COURT OF CHARLES II. With some Account of their Surroundings. With 15 Portraits. 8vo. 16s.

FALKLANDS. With 6 Portraits and 2 other Illustrations. 8vo. 10s. 6d.

THE LIFE OF SIR KENELM DIGBY : By One of his Descendants. With 7 Illustrations. 8vo. 16s.

THE ADVENTURES OF KING JAMES II. OF ENGLAND.   With an Introduction by the Right Rev. F. A. GASQUET, D.D. With 27 Portraits and other Illustrations.   8vo. 13s. 6d. *net.*

CHISEL, PEN AND POIGNARD : Or, Benvenuto Cellini, his Times and his Contemporaries. With 19 Illustrations. Crown 8vo. 5s.

MARSHAL TURENNE. With an Introduction by Brigadier-General FRANCIS LLOYD, C.B., D.S.O. With numerous Illustrations. 8vo. 12s. 6d. *net.*

Biography, etc.

CONFESSIONS OF A CONVERT. By the Very Rev. Monsignor ROBERT HUGH BENSON. Crown 8vo. 3s. 6d. *net*.

This is the record of the author's religious life and development, with accounts of the various stages of belief through which he passed, and of the influences which bore upon him. The book includes sketches of his home education, his school life, his ministry as a parochial clergyman in town and country, his membership in an Anglican Religious community; and finally the stages by which he came to submit to Rome and his experiences in the city itself. The book is not definitely controversial; it is rather narrative and descriptive.

BACK TO HOLY CHURCH: Experiences and Knowledge acquired by a Convert. By Dr. ALBERT VON RUVILLE, Professor of History at the University of Halle, Germany. Translated by G. SCHOETENSACK. Edited with a Preface by the Very Rev. Monsignor ROBERT HUGH BENSON. With Portrait. Crown 8vo. 3s. 6d. *net*.

APOLOGIA PRO VITA SUA, being a History of his Religious Opinions. By JOHN HENRY CARDINAL NEWMAN. Crown 8vo. 3s. 6d.

Pocket Edition. Fcap. 8vo, cloth, 2s. 6d. *net*; leather, 3s. 6d. *net*.

Popular Edition, 8vo, paper covers, 6d. *net*.

The "Pocket" Edition and the "Popular" Edition of this book contain a letter, hitherto unpublished, written by Cardinal Newman to Canon Flanagan in 1857, which may be said to contain in embryo the "Apologia" itself.

THE LIFE OF JOHN HENRY CARDINAL NEWMAN. Based on his Private Journals and Correspondence. By WILFRID WARD. With 2 Portraits. 2 vols. 8vo. 12s. 6d. *net*.

THE LIFE AND TIMES OF CARDINAL WISEMAN. By WILFRID WARD. With 3 Portraits. 2 vols. Crown 8vo. 10s. *net*.

WILLIAM GEORGE WARD AND THE CATHOLIC REVIVAL. By WILFRID WARD. With a New Preface, Portrait and Facsimile. 8vo. 6s. 6d. *net*.

TEN PERSONAL STUDIES. By WILFRID WARD. With 10 Portraits. 8vo. 10s. 6d. *net*.

CONTENTS.—Arthur James Balfour—Three Notable Editors: Delane, Hutton, Knowles—Some Characteristics of Henry Sidgwick—Robert, Earl of Lytton—Father Ignatius Ryder—Sir M. E. Grant Duff's Diaries—Leo XIII.—The Genius of Cardinal Wiseman—John Henry Newman—Newman and Manning—Appendix

ESSAYS ON MEN AND MATTERS. By WILFRID WARD. 8vo.

CONTENTS.—Disraeli—Lord Cromer on Disraeli—G. K. Chesterton as a Prophet—John Stuart Mill—Tennyson at Freshwater—Cardinal Vaughan—The Sensitiveness of Cardinal Newman—Papers read before the Synthetic Society, and other Essays.

ESSAYS. By the Rev. FATHER IGNATIUS DUDLEY RYDER. Edited by FRANCIS BACCHUS, of the Oratory, Birmingham. With Frontispiece. 8vo. 9s. *net*.

For Contents see page 14.

Biography, etc.—*continued*.

LIVES OF THE ENGLISH MARTYRS.

First Series. THE MARTYRS DECLARED BLESSED BY POPE LEO XIII. Edited by DOM BEDE CAMM, O.S.B. Crown 8vo. 7s. 6d. *net* each.

Vol. I. MARTYRS UNDER KING HENRY VIII. (1535-1545).
Vol. II. MARTYRS UNDER QUEEN ELIZABETH (1570-1583).

Second Series. THE MARTYRS DECLARED VENERABLE. Edited by EDWIN H. BURTON, D.D., and JOHN H. POLLEN, S.J.

Vol. I. 1583-1588. Crown 8vo. 7s. 6d. *net*.

THE THREE SISTERS OF LORD RUSSELL OF
KILLOWEN AND THEIR CONVENT LIFE. By the Rev. MATTHEW RUSSELL, S.J. With 5 Illustrations. 8vo. 6s. *net*.

UNSEEN FRIENDS. By Mrs. WILLIAM O'BRIEN.
With a Photogravure Portrait of Nano Nagle, Foundress of the Presentation Order. 8vo. 6s. 6d. *net*.

For Contents see page 14.

AUBREY DE VERE: a Memoir based on his unpublished
Diaries and Correspondence. By WILFRID WARD. With Two Photogravure Portraits and 2 other Illustrations. 8vo. 14s. *net*.

THE HISTORY OF ST. CATHERINE OF SIENA
AND HER COMPANIONS. With a Translation of her Treatise on Consummate Perfection. By AUGUSTA THEODOSIA DRANE. With 10 Illustrations. 2 vols. 8vo. 15s.

A MEMOIR OF MOTHER FRANCIS RAPHAEL,
O.S.D. (AUGUSTA THEODOSIA DRANE), sometime Prioress Provincial of the Congregation of Dominican Sisters of St. Catherine of Siena, Stone. With some of her Spiritual Notes and Letters. Edited by the Rev. Father BERTRAND WILBERFORCE, O.P. With portrait. Crown 8vo. 7s. 6d.

LIFE OF THE MARQUISE DE LA ROCHE-
JAQUELEIN, THE HEROINE OF LA VENDÉE. By the Hon. Mrs. MAXWELL SCOTT (of Abbotsford). With 8 Illustrations and a Map. 8vo. 7s. 6d. *net*.

LIFE OF ST. FRANCIS OF ASSISI. By Father
CUTHBERT, O.S.F.C. With 13 Illustrations. 8vo. 12s. 6d. *net*.

SAINT FRANCIS OF ASSISI: a Biography. By
JOHANNES JÖRGENSEN. Translated by T. O'CONOR SLOANE. With 5 Illustrations. 8vo. 12s. 6d. *net*.

THE LIFE AND LEGEND OF THE LADY SAINT
CLARE: Translated from the French version (1563) of Brother Francis du Puis. By Mrs. REGINALD BALFOUR. With an Introduction by Father CUTHBERT, O.S.F.C., and 24 Illustrations. Crown 8vo. Gilt top. 4s. 6d *net*.

Biography, etc.—*continued.*

LIFE OF ST. ELIZABETH OF HUNGARY,

DUCHESS OF THURINGIA. By the COUNT DE MONTALEM-BERT, Peer of France, Member of the French Academy. Translated by FRANCIS DEMING HOYT. Large Crown 8vo. 10s. 6d. *net.*

LIFE OF THE VISCOUNTESS DE BONNAULT

D'HOUET, Foundress of the Society of the Faithful Companions of Jesus, 1781-1858. By the Rev. FATHER STANISLAUS, F.M., Capuchin of the Province of Paris. Translated from the French by one of her daughters. With Prefaces by His Eminence CARDINAL BOURNE, Archbish:p of W stminster ; and by the Right Rev. ABBOT GASQUET, President of the English Benedictines. With Pho ogravure Portrait and 57 Illustrations. 8vo. Quarter bound, gilt top, 7s. 6d. *net ;* Superior binding, full leather, gilt edges, 21s. *net.*

HISTORY OF ST. VINCENT DE PAUL, Founder of

the Congregation of the Mission (Vincentians), and of the Sisters of Charity. By Monseigneur BOUGAUD, Bishop of Laval. Translated from the Second French Edition by the Rev. JOSEPH BRADY, C.M. With an Introduction by His Eminence CARDINAL VAUGHAN, late Arch-bishop of Westminster. Crown 8vo. 4s. 6d. *net.*

IN ST. DOMINIC'S COUNTRY. By C. M. ANTONY.

Edited with a Preface by the Rev. T. M. SCHWERTNER, O.P., S.T.L. With 50 Illustrations. Crown 8vo. 6s. *net.*

The record of a pilgrimage to the towns and villages of Southern France known to have been visited by Saint Dominic, between 1205-1219, with the account of his Apostolate there, and the founding of his First and Second Orders. A sketch of the Albigensian Crusade is also given. The book is illustrated with over forty photographs, more than half of which have been expressly taken for the purpose, and contains two sketch maps. It may on this account fairly lay claim to be—at least for these fourteen important years—a Picture Book of Saint Dominic.

The Beginnings of the Church.

A Series of Histories of the First Century.

By the Abbé CONSTANT FOUARD, Honorary Cathedral Canon Professor of the Faculty of Theology at Rouen, etc., etc.

THE CHRIST, THE SON OF GOD. A Life of Our

Lord and Saviour Jesus Christ. With an Introduction by CARDINAL MANNING. With 3 Maps. Two vols. Crown 8vo. 14s.

Popular Edition. 8vo. Cloth, 1s. *net.* Paper Covers, 6d. *net.*

ST. PETER AND THE FIRST YEARS OF CHRIS-

TIANITY. With 3 Maps. Crown 8vo. 9s.

ST. PAUL AND HIS MISSIONS. With 2 Maps. Crown

8vo. 9s.

Popular Edition. 8vo. Cloth, 1s. *net.* Paper Covers, 6d. *net.*

THE LAST YEARS OF ST. PAUL. With 5 Maps

and Plans. Crown 8vo. 9s.

ST. JOHN AND THE CLOSE OF THE APOSTOLIC

ACE. Crown 8vo. 7s. 6d.

Lives of the Friar Saints.

Editors for the Franciscan Lives :
The Very Rev. Fr. OSMUND COONEY, O.F.M., Provincial, and
C. M. ANTONY.

Editors for the Dominican Lives :
The Rev. Fr. BEDE JARRETT, O.P., and C. M. ANTONY.
Fcap. 8vo. Cloth, 1s. 6d. per volume ; Leather, 2s. 6d. *net* per volume.

THE HOLY FATHER has expressed through the Very Rev. Fr. Thomas Esser, O.P., Secretary of the Congregation of the Index, his great pleasure and satisfaction that the series has been undertaken, and wishes it every success. He bestows "most affectionately" His Apostolic Blessing upon the Editors, Writers, and Readers of the whole series.

The Master-General of the Dominicans, at Rome, in sending his blessing to the writers and readers of the series, says : " The Lives should teach their readers not only to know the Saints, but also to imitate them ".

The Minister-General of the Franciscans sends his blessing and best wishes for the success of the series.

The series, which has received the warm approval of the authorities of both Orders in England, Ireland, and America, is earnestly recommended to Tertiaries, and to the Catholic public generally.

Fr. OSMUND COONEY, O.F.M.,
Fr. BEDE JARRETT, O.P.,
C. M. ANTONY,
Editors.

DOMINICAN.

ST. THOMAS AQUINAS.
Of the Order of Preachers (1225-1274). A Biographical Study of the Angelic Doctor. By Fr. PLACID CONWAY, O.P. With 5 Illustrations.

ST. VINCENT FERRER,
O.P. By Fr. STANISLAUS HOGAN, O.P. With 4 Illustrations.

ST. PIUS V. Pope of the
Holy Rosary. By C. M. ANTONY. With Preface by the Very Rev. Monsignor BENSON. With 4 Illustrations.

FRANCISCAN.

ST. BONAVENTURE.
The Seraphic Doctor. Minister General of the Franciscan Order, Cardinal Bishop of Albano. By Fr. LAURENCE COSTELLOE, O.F.M. With 6 Illustrations.

ST. ANTONY OF PADUA.
The Miracle Worker (1195-1231). By C. M. ANTONY. With 4 Illustrations.

ST. JOHN CAPISTRAN.
By Fr. VINCENT FITZGERALD, O.F.M. With 4 Illustrations.

Belles Lettres.

LEVIA PONDERA: An Essay Book. By JOHN AYSCOUGH. Crown 8vo, 5s. *net.*

CONTENTS.—Sir Walter—A Scamp's Probation—" The Entail ": an Appreciation—The Leddy o' Grippy—Fickle Fame—King's Servants—An Essay on Essayists—Parallels—Loyalists and Patriots—Time's Reprisals—Cause and Cure—The Shoe and the Foot—Of Old Ways—Scientiae Inimici—Laxity or Sanctity—Press and Public—On Book Buying—Of Dislike of Books—Atmosphere and Antidote—On Sitting Still—Diabolica Trees—Footnotes —" This Public Conscience "—State and Conscience—Empire Day—Duty and Discipline—On Decadence—Messrs. Hooligan and Turveydrop—Two Pessimisms—Peace and Peoples —Dress and Clothing—Of Cathedrals—Of Stone Sermons and White Elephants—An Admiration Note—Why Norwich ?—Cold Porridge—Of Weaker Brethren—The Roman Road —Of Saints and Worthies—Of Great Age—Mare's Nests and Much Boasting—Of Lapse and Losses.

IN GOD'S NURSERY. By C. C. MARTINDALE, S.J. Crown 8vo. 3s. 6d. *net.*

These are sketches of children's lives as they have been lived at different times, and in different parts of God's great Nursery, the world. They are touched in with a light hand, and thus justify the quotation that " The Streets of the City shall be full of Boys and Girls playing in the Streets thereof ".

HAPPINESS AND BEAUTY. By the Right Rev. JOHN S. VAUGHAN, D.D., Bishop of Sebastopolis. Crown 8vo. 1s. 6d. *net.*

CONTENTS.—The Hunger of the Heart—Certain Leading Principles—Various Degrees of Happiness—Man's Magnificent Destiny—Beauty : Visible and Invisible.

ESSAYS. By the Rev. FATHER IGNATIUS DUDLEY RYDER. Edited by FRANCIS BACCHUS, of the Oratory, Birmingham. With Frontispiece. 8vo. 9s. *net.*

CONTENTS.—A Jesuit Reformer and Poet : Frederick Spee—Revelations of the After-World—Savonarola—M. Emery, Superior of St. Sulpice, 1789-1811—Auricular Confession—The Pope and the Anglican Archbishops—Ritualism, Roman Catholicism, and Converts—On Certain Ecclesiastical Miracles—The Ethics of War—The Passions of the Past—Some Memories of a Jail Chaplain—Purcell's Life of Cardinal Manning.

APPENDIX.—Some Notes on Ryder's Controversy with Ward.

UNSEEN FRIENDS. By Mrs. WILLIAM O'BRIEN. With a Photogravure Portrait of Nano Nagle, Foundress of the Presentation Order. 8vo. 6s. 6d. *net.*

CONTENTS.—Mother Margaret Mary Hallahan—A Novelist of the last Century : Mrs. Oliphant—Nano Nagle—Charlotte Brontë at Home—Mary Aikenhead, Foundress of the Irish Sisters of Charity—Felicia Skene—Catharine McAuley, Foundress of the Sisters of Mercy—Jean Ingelow—Mother Frances Raphael Drane—Eugénie de Guérin—Emilie d'Oultrement—Pauline de la Ferronays and her Family—A French Heroine in China : Hélène de Jaurias, Sister of Charity—Christina Rossetti—Marie Antoniette Fage.

A GUIDE TO BOOKS ON IRELAND. By STEPHEN J. BROWN, S.J. 3 vols. Crown 8vo.

Vol. I. PROSE, LITERATURE, POETRY, MUSIC, and PLAYS. 6s. *net.*

Vols. II. and III. *In preparation.*

For Spiritual Reading.

THE SERMON OF THE SEA, and Other Studies. By the Rev. ROBERT KANE, S.J. Crown 8vo. 5s. *net.*

THE PLAIN GOLD RING. By the Rev. ROBERT KANE, S.J. Crown 8vo. 2s. 6d. *net.*

GOOD FRIDAY TO EASTER SUNDAY. By the Rev. ROBERT KANE, S.J. Crown 8vo. 2s. 6d. *net.*

SERMONS AND HOMILIES. By the Rev. EDMUND ENGLISH, Canon of Westminster Cathedral and Missionary Rector of St. James's, Twickenham. Crown 8vo. 4s. *net.*

AT HOME WITH GOD : Priedieu Papers on Spiritual Subjects. By the Rev. MATTHEW RUSSELL, S.J. Crown 8vo. 3s. 6d. *net.*

AMONG THE BLESSED : Loving Thoughts about Favourite Saints. By the Rev. MATTHEW RUSSELL, S.J. With 8 full-page Illustrations. Crown 8vo. 3s. 6d. *net.*

THE PARADOXES OF CATHOLICISM. Sermons preached in Rome, Easter, 1913. By the Very Rev. Monsignor ROBERT HUGH BENSON. Crown 8vo. 3s. 6d. *net.*

CHRIST IN THE CHURCH : A Volume of Religious Essays. By the Very Rev. Monsignor ROBERT HUGH BENSON. Crown 8vo. 3s. 6d. *net.*

THE FRIENDSHIP OF CHRIST : Sermons. By the Very Rev. Monsignor ROBERT HUGH BENSON. Crown 8vo. 3s. 6d. *net.*

SELF-KNOWLEDGE AND SELF-DISCIPLINE. By the Rev. B. W. MATURIN. Crown 8vo. 5s. *net.*

LAWS OF THE SPIRITUAL LIFE. By the Rev. B. W. MATURIN. Crown 8vo. 5s. *net.*

SPIRITUAL GLEANINGS FOR MARIAN SODAL-ISTS. By MADAME CECILIA, Religious of St. Andrew's Convent, Streatham, London, S.W. With a Frontispiece. Crown 8vo, 2s. 6d. *net.*

THE INNER LIFE OF THE SOUL. Short Spiritual Messages for the Ecclesiastical Year. By S. L. EMERY. Crown 8vo. 4s. 6d. *net.*

THESAURUS FIDELIUM : a Manual for those who desire to lead Prayerful Lives in the World. Compiled by a CARMELITE TERTIARY (H. M. K.). Fcap 8vo.

OUR LADY IN THE CHURCH, and other Essays. By M. NESBITT. With a Preface by the Right Rev. Dr. CASARTELLI, Bishop of Salford. With a Frontispiece. Crown 8vo. 4s. 6d. *net.*

A collection of essays, mainly historical or antiquarian in character. The papers deal with the life and work of the Catholic Church, and with various manners, customs, and religious observances in mediæval times.

For Young People.

THE HOUSE AND TABLE OF GOD: a Book for His Children Young and Old. By the Rev. WILLIAM ROCHE, S.J. With 24 Drawings by T. BAINES. Crown 8vo. Cloth, 2s. 6d. *net*; Vegetable Vellum, 3s. 6d. *net*.

This book is primarily intended to guide the thoughts of children at an age when they begin to wonder, and to argue secretly within themselves about questions of life and religion; but is equally suited to the open-minded of every age. It offers a consecutive series of readings calculated to deepen religious thought and feeling on essential truth.

A CHILD'S RULE OF LIFE. By the Very Rev. Monsignor ROBERT HUGH BENSON. Printed in Red and Black and Illustrated by GABRIEL PIPPET. 4to. Paper Covers, 1s. *net*; Cloth, 2s. *net*.

OLD TESTAMENT RHYMES. By the Very Rev. Monsignor ROBERT HUGH BENSON. Printed in Red and Black, and Illustrated by GABRIEL PIPPET. 4to. Paper Covers, 1s. *net*; Cloth, 2s. *net*.

A LIFE OF CHRIST FOR CHILDREN. With 20 Illustrations, reproduced chiefly from the Old Masters. With Preface by His Eminence CARDINAL GIBBONS. Large Crown 8vo. 4s. *net*.

BIBLE STORIES TOLD TO "TODDLES". By Mrs. HERMANN BOSCH. Crown 8vo. 2s. 6d. *net*.

WHEN "TODDLES" WAS SEVEN: A Sequel to "Bible Stories told to 'Toddles'". By Mrs. HERMANN BOSCH. Crown 8vo. 3s. *net*.

THE GOOD SHEPHERD AND HIS LITTLE LAMBS. By Mrs. HERMANN BOSCH. With a Frontispiece. Fcap. 8vo. 2s. 6d. *net*.

STORIES ON THE ROSARY. By LOUISE EMILY DOBRÉE. Parts I., II., III. Crown 8vo. 1s. 6d. each.

OLD RHYMES WITH NEW TUNES. Composed by RICHARD RUNCIMAN TERRY, Mus. Doc., F.R.C.O., Organist and Director of the Choir at Westminster Cathedral. With Illustrations by GABRIEL PIPPET. 4to. 2s. 6d. *net*.

A MYSTERY PLAY IN HONOUR OF THE NATIVITY OF OUR LORD. By the Very Rev. Monsignor ROBERT HUGH BENSON. With 14 Illustrations by GABRIEL PIPPET; Appendices, and Stage Directions. Crown 8vo. 2s. 6d. *net*. Acting Edition. 6d. *net*.

THE COST OF A CROWN: a Story of Douay and Durham. A Sacred Drama in Three Acts. By the Very Rev. Monsignor ROBERT HUGH BENSON. With 9 Illustrations by GABRIEL PIPPET. Crown 8vo. 3s. 6d. *net*.

THE MAID OF ORLEANS. By the Very Rev. Monsignor ROBERT HUGH BENSON. With 14 Illustrations by GABRIEL PIPPET. Crown 8vo. 3s. *net*. Acting Edition. 6d. *net*.

Poetry and Romance.

WELSH POETRY (OLD AND NEW) IN ENGLISH
VERSE. By ALFRED PERCEVAL GRAVES, M.A. ("Canwr Cilarné"). Crown 8vo. 2s. 6d.

BALLADS OF IRISH CHIVALRY. By ROBERT
DWYER JOYCE, M.D. Edited, with Annotations, by his brother, P. W. JOYCE, LL.D. With Portrait of the Author and 3 Illustrations. 8vo. Cloth gilt, 2s. *net.* Paper Covers, 1s. *net.*

OLD CELTIC ROMANCES. Twelve of the most beauti-
ful of the Ancient Irish Romantic Tales. Translated from the Gaelic. By P. W. JOYCE, LL.D., M.R.I.A. Crown 8vo. 3s. 6d.

ANCIENT IRISH MUSIC. Containing One Hundred
Airs never before published, and a number of Popular Songs. Collected and Edited by P. W. JOYCE, LL.D., M.R.I.A. 4to. Paper wrappers, 1s. 6d. Cloth, 3s.

OLD IRISH FOLK MUSIC AND SONGS: a collection
of 842 Irish Airs and Songs hitherto unpublished. Edited by P. W. JOYCE, LL.D., M.R.I.A., with Annotations, for the Royal Society of Antiquaries of Ireland. Medium 8vo. 10s. 6d. *net.*

IRISH PEASANT SONGS. In the English Language;
the words set to the proper Old Irish Airs. Collected and Edited by P. W. JOYCE, LL.D., M.R.I.A. Crown 8vo. Paper Covers, 6d. *net.*

HISTORICAL BALLAD POETRY OF IRELAND.
Arranged by M. J. BROWN. With an Introduction by STEPHEN J. BROWN, S.J. With 8 Portraits. Crown 8vo. 3s. 6d.

Fiction.

GRACECHURCH. By JOHN AYSCOUGH. Crown 8vo. 6s.

A READER'S GUIDE TO IRISH FICTION. By STEPHEN J. BROWN, S.J. Crown 8vo. 3s. 6d. *net.*

THE FUGITIVES. By MARGARET FLETCHER. Crown 8vo. 6s.

CATHERINE SIDNEY. By FRANCIS DEMING HOYT. Crown 8vo. 6s.

Novels by Mrs. Wilfrid Ward.

ONE POOR SCRUPLE. Crown 8vo. 6s.

OUT OF DUE TIME. Crown 8vo. 6s.

GREAT POSSESSIONS. Crown 8vo. 6s.

THE LIGHT BEHIND. Crown 8vo. 6s.

THE JOB SECRETARY. An Impression. Crown 8vo. 4s. 6d.

Novels by M. E. Francis (Mrs. Francis Blundell).

CHRISTIAN THAL. With Musical Chapter Headings. Crown 8vo. 6s.

DORSET DEAR: Idylls of Country Life. Crown 8vo. 6s.

LYCHGATE HALL: a Romance. Crown 8vo. 6s.

THE MANOR FARM. With Frontispiece by Claude C. du Pré Cooper. Crown 8vo. 6s.

FIANDER'S WIDOW. Crown 8vo. 6s.

YEOMAN FLEETWOOD. Crown 8vo. 3s. *net.*

Works by the Very Rev. Canon Sheehan, D.D.

MIRIAM LUCAS. A Story of Irish Life. Crown 8vo. 6s.

THE QUEEN'S FILLET. A Tale of the French Revolution. Crown 8vo. 6s.

LISHEEN; or, The Test of the Spirits. A Novel. Cr. 8vo. 6s.

LUKE DELMEGE. A Novel. Crown 8vo. 6s.

GLENANAAR: a Story of Irish Life. Crown 8vo. 6s.

THE BLINDNESS OF DR. GRAY; or, the Final Law: a Novel of Clerical Life. Crown 8vo. 6s.

"LOST ANGEL OF A RUINED PARADISE": a Drama of Modern Life. Crown 8vo. 3s. 6d.

THE INTELLECTUALS : An Experiment in Irish Club Life. 8vo. 6s.

PARERGA: being a Companion Volume to "Under the Cedars and the Stars". Crown 8vo. 7s. 6d. *net.*

EARLY ESSAYS AND LECTURES. Crown 8vo. 6s. *net.*

CONTENTS.

Essays.	*Lectures.*
Religious Instruction in Intermediate Schools—In a Dublin Art Gallery—Emerson—Free-Thought in America—German Universities (Three Essays)—German and Gallic Muses—Augustinian Literature—The Poetry of Matthew Arnold—Recent Works on St. Augustine—Aubrey de Vere (a Study).	Irish Youth and High Ideals—The Two Civilisations—The Golden Jubilee of O'Connell's Death—Our Personal and Social Responsibilities—The Study of Mental Science—Certain Elements of Character—The Limitations and Possibilities of Catholic Literature.

Education.

A HISTORY OF ENGLAND FOR CATHOLIC SCHOOLS. By E. WYATT-DAVIES, M.A. With 14 Maps. Crown 8vo. 3s. 6d.

OUTLINES OF BRITISH HISTORY. By E. WYATT-DAVIES, M.A. With 85 Illustrations and 13 Maps. Crown 8vo. 2s. 6d.

A CHILD'S HISTORY OF IRELAND. From the Earliest Times to the Death of O'Connell. By P. W. JOYCE, LL.D., M.R.I.A. With specially constructed Map and 160 Illustrations, including Facsimile in Full Colours of an Illuminated Page of the Gospel Book of MacDurnan, A.D. 850. Fcp. 8vo. 3s. 6d.

OUTLINES OF THE HISTORY OF IRELAND. From the Earliest Times to 1905. By P. W. JOYCE, LL.D., M.R.I.A. Fcp. 8vo. 9d.

A READING BOOK IN IRISH HISTORY. By P. W. JOYCE, LL.D., M.R.I.A. With 45 Illustrations. Crown 8vo. 1s. 6d.

A HISTORY OF IRELAND FOR AUSTRALIAN CATHOLIC SCHOOLS. From the Earliest Times to the Death of O'Connell. By P. W. JOYCE, LL.D., M.R.I.A. With specially constructed Map and 160 Illustrations, including Facsimile in Full Colours of an Illuminated Page of the Gospel Book of MacDurnan, A.D. 850. Fcap. 8vo. 2s.

The authorised Irish History for Catholic Schools and Colleges throughout Australasia.

AN EXPERIMENT IN HISTORY TEACHING. By EDWARD ROCKLIFF, S.J. With 3 Coloured Charts. Crown 8vo. 2s. 6d. *net.*

HISTORICAL ATLAS OF INDIA, for the Use of High Schools, Colleges and Private Students. By CHARLES JOPPEN, S.J. 29 Maps in Colours. Post 4to. 2s. 6d.

GRAMMAR LESSONS. By the PRINCIPAL OF ST. MARY'S HALL, Liverpool. Crown 8vo. 2s.

THE CLASS TEACHING OF ENGLISH COMPOSITION. By the PRINCIPAL OF ST. MARY'S HALL, Liverpool. Crown 8vo. 2s.

ENGLISH AS WE SPEAK IT IN IRELAND. By P. W. JOYCE, LL.D., M.R.I.A. Crown 8vo. 2s. 6d. *net.*

A GRAMMAR OF THE IRISH LANGUAGE. By P. W. JOYCE, LL.D., M.R.I.A. Fcp. 8vo. 1s.

STUDIES IN THE HISTORY OF CLASSICAL TEACHING. By the Rev. T. CORCORAN, S.J. Crown 8vo. 7s. 6d. *net.*

Education—*continued.*

HANDBOOK OF HOMERIC STUDY. By HENRY BROWNE, S.J., M.A., New College, Oxford. With 22 Plates. Crown 8vo. 6s. *net.*

HANDBOOK OF GREEK COMPOSITION. With Exercises for Junior and Middle Classes. By HENRY BROWNE, S.J., M.A. Crown 8vo. 3s. *net.*

Key for the Use of Masters only, 5s. 2d. *net.*

HANDBOOK OF LATIN COMPOSITION. With Exercises. By HENRY BROWNE, S.J., M.A. Crown 8vo. 3s. *net.*

Key for the Use of Masters only, 5s. 2d. *net.*

SCIENCE OF EDUCATION. By T. P. KEATING, B.A., L.C.P. With an Introduction by Rev. T. A. FINLAY, M.A., National University, Dublin. Crown 8vo. 2s. 6d. *net.*

THE EDUCATION OF CATHOLIC GIRLS. By JANET ERSKINE STUART. With a Preface by the CARDINAL ARCHBISHOP OF WESTMINSTER. Crown 8vo. 3s. 6d. *net.*

THE TEACHER'S COMPANION. By Brother DE SALES, M.A. Diplomate in Education, etc. Crown 8vo. 2s. 6d. *net.*

₊ *A book on School Methods, with blank pages for the insertion of the personal experiences of the teacher.*

A HANDBOOK OF SCHOOL MANAGEMENT AND METHODS OF TEACHING. By P. W. JOYCE, LL.D., M.R.I.A. Fcp. 3s. 6d.

QUICK AND DEAD? To Teachers. By Two of Them. Crown 8vo. 1s. 6d.

THE FOUNTAIN OF LIFE. To Catholic Teachers. By One of the Authors of "Quick and Dead". Crown 8vo. 1s. *net.*

PRINCIPLES OF LOGIC. By G. H. JOYCE, S.J., M.A., Oxford, Professor of Logic at Stonyhurst. 8vo. 6s. 6d. *net.*

INTRODUCTORY PHILOSOPHY: a Textbook for Colleges and High Schools. By CHARLES A. DUBRAY, S.M., Ph.D., Professor of Philosophy at the Marist College, Washington, D.C. With a Preface by Professor E. D. PACE, of the Catholic University, Washington, D.C. 8vo. 10s. 6d. *net.*

FIVE CENTURIES OF ENGLISH POETRY. From Chaucer to De Vere. Representative Selections with Notes and Remarks on the Art of Reading Verse Aloud. By the Rev. GEORGE O'NEILL, S.J., M.A., Professor of English, University College, Dublin. Crown 8vo. 3s. 6d. *net.*

Cardinal Newman's Works.

1. SERMONS.

PAROCHIAL AND PLAIN SERMONS. Edited by the Rev. W. J. COPELAND, B.D. 8 vols. Crown 8vo. 3s. 6d. each.

The first six volumes are reprinted from the six volumes of *Parochial Sermons*, first published in 1834, 1835, 1836, 1838, 1840, and 1842 respectively; the seventh and eighth formed the fifth volume of **Plain Sermons by Contributors to the Tracts for the Times**, originally published in 1843.

The fame of these sermons has been celebrated by Froude, Principal Shairp. James Mozley, Dean Church, and others. "The Tracts," writes the last-named in his *Oxford Movement*, "were not the most powerful instruments in drawing sympathy to the movement. None but those who heard them can adequately estimate the effect of Mr. Newman's four o'clock sermons at St. Mary's. The world knows them . . . but it hardly realizes that without these sermons the movement might never have gone on. . . . While men were reading and talking about the Tracts, they were hearing the sermons; and in the sermons they heard the living meaning, and reason, and bearing of the Tracts. . . . The sermons created a moral atmosphere, in which men judged the questions in debate." The *Parochial Sermons* fell out of print between 1845 and 1868, at which latter date they were republished by Newman's former curate at St. Mary's, Mr. Copeland. The success of this re-issue was a striking testimony to the degree to which Newman had recovered his popularity and prestige by the Apologia. He recorded in his private journal that in six months 3500 copies of the first volume were sold.

Ward's *Life of Newman*, vol. ii. p. 241.

SELECTION, ADAPTED TO THE SEASONS OF THE ECCLESIASTICAL YEAR, from the "Parochial and Plain Sermons". Edited by the Rev. W. J. COPELAND, B.D. Crown 8vo. 3s. 6d.

This volume consisting of fifty-four sermons was first published in 1878.

CONTENTS:—*Advent:* Self-denial the Test of Religious Earnestness—Divine Calls—The Ventures of Faith—Watching. *Christmas Day:* Religious Joy. *New Year's Sunday:* The Lapse of Time—*Epiphany:* Remembrance of Past Mercies—Equanimity—The Immortality of the Soul—Christian Manhood—Sincerity and Hypocrisy—Christian Sympathy. *Septuagesima:* Present Blessings. *Sexagesima:* Endurance, the Christian's Portion. *Quinquagesima:* Love, the One Thing Needful. *Lent:* The Individuality of the Soul—Life, the Season of Repentance—Bodily Suffering—Tears of Christ at the Grave of Lazarus—Christ's Privations, a Meditation for Christians—The Cross of Christ the Measure of the World. *Good Friday:* The Crucifixion. *Easter Day.* Keeping Fast and Festival. *Easter Tide:* Witnesses of the Resurrection—A Particular Providence as revealed in the Gospel—Christ Manifested in Remembrance—The Invisible World—Waiting for Christ. *Ascension:* Warfare the Condition of Victory. *Sunday after Ascension:* Rising with Christ. *Whitsun Day:* The Weapons of Saints. *Trinity Sunday:* The Mysteriousness of Our Present Being. *Sundays after Trinity:* Holiness Necessary for Future Blessedness—The Religious Use of Excited Feelings—The Self-wise Inquirer—Scripture a Record of Human Sorrow—The Danger of Riches—Obedience without Love, as instanced in the Character of Balaam—Moral Consequences of Single Sins—The Greatness and Littleness of Human Life—Moral Effects of Communion with God—The Thought of God the Stay of the Soul—The Power of the Will—The Gospel Palaces—Religion a Weariness to the Natural Man—The World our Enemy—The Praise of Men—Religion Pleasant to the Religious—Mental Prayer—Curiosity a Temptation to Sin—Miracles no Remedy for Unbelief—Jeremiah, a Lesson for the Disappointed—The Shepherd of our Souls—Doing Glory to God in Pursuits of the World.

Cardinal Newman's Works—*continued.*

SERMONS BEARING UPON SUBJECTS OF THE
DAY. Edited by the Rev. W. J. COPELAND, B.D. Crown 8vo. 3s. 6d.

This volume was first published in 1843, and republished by Mr. Copeland in 1869. This collection contains the celebrated sermons " Wisdom and Innocence," and " The Parting of Friends ". Mr. Copeland appended to it very important chronological lists, giving the dates at which the sermons contained in it and the eight volumes of *Parochial and Plain Sermons* were first delivered.

CONTENTS.—The Work of the Christian—Saintliness not Forfeited by the Penitent—Our Lord's Last Supper and His First—Dangers to the Penitent—The Three Offices of Christ—Faith and Experience—Faith unto the World—The Church and the World—Indulgence in Religious Privileges—Connection between Personal and Public Improvement—Christian Nobleness—Joshua a Type of Christ and His Followers—Elisha a Type of Christ and His Followers—The Christian Church a Continuation of the Jewish—The Principles of Continuity between the Jewish and Christian Churches—The Christian Church an Imperial Power—Sanctity the Token of the Christian Empire—Condition of the Members of the Christian Empire—The Apostolic Christian—Wisdom and Innocence —Invisible Presence of Christ—Outward and Inward Notes of the Church—Grounds for Steadfastness in our Religious Profession—Elijah the Prophet of the Latter Days—Feasting in Captivity—The Parting of Friends.

FIFTEEN SERMONS PREACHED BEFORE THE
UNIVERSITY OF OXFORD, between 1826 and 1843. Cr. 8vo. 3s. 6d.

The first edition of these sermons was published in 1843 ; the second in 1844. The original title was " Sermons, chiefly on the Theory of Religious Belief, Preached," etc. The third edition was published in 1870, with (1) a new Preface, in which the author explains, *inter alia*, the sense in which he had used the term " Reason" in the sermons ; and (2) notes " to draw attention to certain faults which are to be found in them, either of thought or language, and, as far as possible, to set these right ". This preface and the notes are of great value to students of the Grammar of Assent. Among the sermons contained in this volume is the celebrated one delivered in 1843 on " The Theory of Developments in Religious Doctrine ".

CONTENTS.—The Philosophical Temper, first enjoined by the Gospel—The Influence of Natural and Revealed Religion respectively—Evangelical Sanctity the Perfection of Natural Virtue—The Usurpations of Reason—Personal Influence, the Means of Propagating the Truth—On Justice as a Principle of Divine Governance—Contest between Faith and Sight—Human Responsibility, as independent of Circumstances—Wilfulness, the Sin of Saul—Faith and Reason, contrasted as Habits of Mind—The Nature of Faith in Relation to Reason—Love, the Safeguard of Faith against Superstition—Implicit and Explicit Reason—Wisdom, as contrasted with Faith and with Bigotry—The Theory of Developments in Religious Doctrine.

DISCOURSES TO MIXED CONGREGATIONS.
Crown 8vo. 3s. 6d.

First published in 1849.

" These sermons have a definite tone and genius of their own . . . and though they have not to me quite the delicate charm of the reserve, and I might almost say the shy passion, of his Oxford sermons, they represent the full-blown blossom of his genius, while the former shows it only in the bud. . . . The extraordinary wealth of detail with which Newman conceives and realises the various sins and miseries of the human lot has, perhaps, never been illustrated in all his writings with so much force as in the wonderful sixteenth sermon on ' The Mental Sufferings of our Lord in His Passion,' " etc.

The late Mr. R. H. HUTTON.

CONTENTS.—The Salvation of the Hearer the Motive of the Preacher—Neglect of Divine Calls and Warnings—Men, not Angels, the Priests of the Gospel—Purity and Love—Saintliness the Standard of Christian Principle—God's Will the End of Life—Perseverance in Grace—Nature and Grace—Illuminating Grace—Faith and Private Judgment—Faith and Doubt—Prospects of the Catholic Missioner—Mysteries of Nature and of Grace—The Mystery of Divine Condescension—The Infinitude of the Divine Attributes—Mental Sufferings of our Lord in His Passion—The Glories of Mary for the Sake of Her Son—On the Fitness of the Glories of Mary.

Cardinal Newman's Works—*continued.*

SERMONS PREACHED ON VARIOUS OCCASIONS. Crown 8vo. 3s. 6d.

This volume, which was first published in 1857, consists of eight sermons preached before the Catholic University of Ireland in 1856-1857, and seven sermons delivered on different occasions between 1850 and 1872. Among the latter are the celebrated " Second Spring " and " The Pope and the Revolution " preached 1850-1872 at St. Chad's, the Oratory, Oscott, and Farm Street, London, with Notes.

CONTENTS.—Intellect the Instrument of Religious Training—The Religion of the Pharisee—The Religion of Mankind—Waiting for Christ—The Secret Power of Divine Grace—Dispositions for Faith—Omnipotence in Bonds—St. Paul's Characteristic Gift —St. Paul's Gift of Sympathy—Christ upon the Waters—The Second Spring—Order, the Witness and Instrument of Unity—The Mission of St. Philip Neri—The Tree beside the Waters—In the World but not of the World—The Pope and the Revolution—Notes.

2. TREATISES.

LECTURES ON THE DOCTRINE OF JUSTIFICATION. Crown 8vo. 3s. 6d.

These Lectures were first published in 1838. They were reprinted in 1874 with an " Advertisement to the Third Edition " and some additional notes.

CONTENTS.—Faith considered as the Instrumental Cause of Justification—Love considered as the Formal Cause of Justification—Primary Sense of the term " Justification "— Secondary Senses of the term " Justification "—Misuse of the term " Just " or " Righteous " —The Gift of Righteousness—The Characteristics of the Gift of Righteousness—Righteousness viewed as a Gift and as a Quality—Righteousness the Fruit of our Lord's Resurrection—The Office of Justifying Faith—The Nature of Justifying Faith—Faith viewed relatively to Rites and Works—On Preaching the Gospel—Appendix—On the Formal Cause of Justification.

AN ESSAY ON THE DEVELOPMENT OF CHRISTIAN DOCTRINE. Crown 8vo. 3s. 6d.

" In this New Edition of the Essay, first published in 1845, various important alterations have been made in the arrangement of its separate parts, and some, not indeed in its matter, but in its text."—*Preface to Third Edition,* 1878.

THE IDEA OF A UNIVERSITY DEFINED AND ILLUSTRATED. Crown 8vo. 3s. 6d.

I. In Nine Discourses delivered to the Catholics of Dublin.
II. In Occasional Lectures and Essays addressed to the members of the Catholic University.

Part I. was first published in 1852 under the title of *Discourses on the Scope an l Nature of University Education, etc.*

CONTENTS.—I. Introductory—II. Theology a Branch of Knowledge—III. Bearing of Theology on other Knowledge—IV. Bearing of other Knowledge on Theology—V. Knowledge its own End—VI. Knowledge viewed in Relation to Learning—VII. Knowledge viewed in Relation to Professional Skill—VIII. Knowledge viewed in Relation to Religious Duty—IX. Duties of the Church towards Knowledge.

Part II. was first published in 1859 under the title of *Lectures and Essays on University Subjects.*

CONTENTS.—I. Christianity and Letters—II. Literature—III. Catholic Literature in the English Tongue—IV. Elementary Studies—V. A Form of Infidelity of the Day—VI. University Preaching—VII. Christianity and Physical Science—VIII. Christianity and Scientific Investigation—IX. Discipline of Mind—X. Christianity and Medical Science.

*** *Part I. is also issued separately as follows :—*

UNIVERSITY TEACHING CONSIDERED IN NINE DISCOURSES. With a Preface by the Rev. JOHN NORRIS. Fcp. 8vo. Cloth, Gilt Top, 2s. *net.* Leather, 3s. *net.*

Cardinal Newman's Works—*continued.*

AN ESSAY IN AID OF A GRAMMAR OF ASSENT.

Crown 8vo. 3s. 6d.

First published in 1870, with Notes at the end of the volume added to the later editions.

AN INDEXED SYNOPSIS OF CARDINAL NEWMAN'S "AN ESSAY IN AID OF A GRAMMAR OF ASSENT".

By the Rev. JOHN J. TOOHEY, S.J. Crown 8vo. 3s. 6d.

3. HISTORICAL.

HISTORICAL SKETCHES. Three vols. Crown 8vo.

3s. 6d. each.

VOL. I.—The Turks in their Relation to Europe—Marcus Tullius Cicero—Apollonius of Tyana—Primitive Christianity.

> The Essay on "The Turks in their Relation to Europe" was first published under the title of *Lectures on the History of the Turks by the Author of Loss and Gain*, in 1854. As is well known, Newman took what was then the unpopular side. The Czar was "attacking an infamous power, the enemy of God and Man". "Many things are possible; one is inconceivable—that the Turks should, as an existing nation, accept of modern civilisation; and in default of it, that they should be able to stand their ground amid the encroachments of Russia, the interested and contemptuous patronage of Europe, and the hatred of their subject populations."

Personal and Literary Character of Cicero. First published in 1824.

Apollonius of Tyana. First published in 1826.

Primitive Christianity.

I. What does St. Ambrose say about it?—II. What says Vincent of Lerins?—III. What says the History of Apollinaris?—IV. What say Jovinian and his companions?—V. What say the Apostolical Canons?

> This series formed part of the original *Church of the Fathers* as it appeared in the *British Magazine* of 1833-36, and as it was published in 1840. "They were removed from subsequent Catholic editions, except the chapter on Apollinaris, as containing polemical matter, which had no interest for Catholic readers. Now [1872] they are republished under a separate title."

VOL. II.—The Church of the Fathers—St. Chrysostom—Theodoret—Mission of St. Benedict—Benedictine Schools.

The Church of the Fathers.

I. Trials of Basil—II. Labours of Basil—III. Basil and Gregory—IV. Rise and Fall of Gregory—V. Antony in Conflict—VI. Antony in Calm—VII. Augustine and the Vandals—VIII. Conversion of Augustine—IX. Demetrias—X. Martin and Maximus.

St. Chrysostom. Reprinted from the *Rambler*, 1859-60.

Trials of Theodoret. First published in 1873.

The Mission of St. Benedict. From the *Atlantis*, 1858.

The Benedictine Schools. From the *Atlantis*, 1859.

VOL. III.—Rise and Progress of Universities (originally published as "Office and Work of Universities")—Northmen and Normans in England and Ireland—Mediæval Oxford—Convocation of Canterbury.

Rise and Progress of Universities.

> The following illustrations of the idea of a University originally appeared in 1854 in the columns of the Dublin *Catholic University Gazette*. In 1856 they were published in one volume under the title of *The Office and Work of Universities, etc.*

Northmen and Normans in England and Ireland. From the *Rambler* of 1859.

Mediaeval Oxford. From the *British Critic* of 1838.

The Convocation of the Province of Canterbury. From the *British Magazine* of 1834-35.

THE CHURCH OF THE FATHERS. Reprinted from "Historical Sketches". Vol. II. With a Preface by the Rev. JOHN NORRIS, Fcp. 8vo. Cloth, Gilt Top. 2s. *net.* Leather. 3s. *net.*

Cardinal Newman's Works—*continued*.

4. ESSAYS.

TWO ESSAYS ON MIRACLES. Crown 8vo. 3s. 6d.

CONTENTS.—I. The Miracles of Scripture compared with those reported elsewhere as regards their nature, credibility, and evidence—II. The Miracles of Early Ecclesiastical History compared with those of Scripture as regards their nature, credibility, and evidence.

The former of these Essays was written for the *Encyclopædia Metropolitana*, 1825-26; the latter in 1842-43 as Preface to a Translation of a portion of Fleury's *Ecclesiastical History*. They were republished in 1870 with some additional notes.

DISCUSSIONS AND ARGUMENTS. Cr. 8vo. 3s. 6d.

1. How to accomplish it. 2. The Antichrist of the Fathers. 3. Scripture and the Creed. 4. Tamworth Reading-room. 5. Who's to Blame? 6. An Internal Argument for Christianity.

How to Accomplish It originally appeared in the *British Magazine* of 1830 under the title of "Home Thoughts Abroad". "The discussion on this Paper is carried on by two speculative Anglicans, who aim at giving vitality to their church, the one by uniting it to the Holy See, the other by developing a nineteenth century Anglo-Catholicism. The narrator sides on the whole with the latter of these."

The Patristical Idea of Antichrist. This was the Eighty-third Number of the *Tracts for the Times*, published in 1838.

Holy Scripture in Its Relation to the Catholic Creed. This was the Eighty-fifth Number of the *Tracts for the Times*.

The Tamworth Reading Room. A series of seven letters, signed "Catholicus," first printed in the *Times* during February, 1841, and published as a pamphlet. They were provoked by addresses delivered by Lord Brougham at Glasgow and Sir Robert Peel at the opening of a Library and Reading Room at Tamworth, in which those distinguished statesmen exalted secular knowledge into the great instrument of moral improvement. They ran as follows: (1) Secular Knowledge in contrast with Religion. (2) Secular Knowledge not the principle of Moral Improvement. (3) Not a direct means of Moral Improvement. (4) Not the antecedent of Moral Improvement. (5) Not a principle of social unity. (6) Not a principle of action. (7) But without personal religion a temptation to unbelief.

Who's to Blame? A series of letters addressed to the *Catholic Standard* in 1855. There was at that time a great deal of blame attributed to the Government on account of its management of the Crimean War. Newman threw the blame on the British constitution, or rather on those who clamoured for a foreign war, for the conduct of which this constitution is singularly ill-adapted. The letters are a valuable study of the genius of the Anglo-Saxon race and the British constitution.

An Internal Argument for Christianity. A review, originally published in the Month of June, 1866, of *Ecce Homo*.

ESSAYS, CRITICAL AND HISTORICAL. Two vols., with Notes. Crown 8vo. 7s.

CONTENTS OF VOL. I.—I. Poetry with reference to Aristotle's Poetics. With Note—II. The Introduction of Rationalistic Principles into Revealed Religion. With Note—III. Apostolical Tradition. With Note—IV. The Fall of la Mennais. With Note—V. Palmer's View of Faith and Unity. With Note—VI. The Theology of St. Ignatius. With Note—VII. Prospects of the Anglican Church. With Note—VIII. The Anglo-American Church. With Note—IX. Selina Countess of Huntingdon. With Note.

CONTENTS OF VOL. II.—X. The Catholicity of the Anglican Church. With Note—XI. The Protestant View of Antichrist. With Note—XII. Milman's View of Christianity. With Note—XIII. The Reformation of the Eleventh Century. With Note—XIV. Private Judgment. With Note—XV. John Davison. With Note—XVI. John Keble. With Note.

The first Essay was written in 1828 for the *London Review*; the second in 1835 for the *Tracts for the Times*; the last in 1846 for the *Dublin Review*; the rest for the *British Critic* between 1837 and 1842. The original title of VII. was *Home Thoughts Abroad*. The "Notes" were written when the Essays were republished in 1871.

Cardinal Newman's Works—*continued.*

5. PATRISTIC.

THE ARIANS OF THE FOURTH CENTURY.
Crown 8vo. 3s. 6d.

First published in 1833. Republished, with an Appendix containing over seventy pages of additional matter, in 1871.

CONTENTS OF APPENDIX.—I. The Syrian School of Theology—II. The Early Doctrine of the Divine Genesis—III. The Confessions at Sirmium—IV. The Early use of *usia* and *hypostasis*—V. Orthodoxy of the Faithful during Arianism—VI. Chronology of the Councils —VII. Omissions in the Text of the Third Edition (1871).

(5) is a long extract from the article published in the *Rambler* of 1859, "On consulting the Faithful on Matters of Doctrine". In the fourth (1876) and subsequent editions of the *Arians* the author appended to the extract an explanation of a passage in the original article which had been seriously misunderstood in some quarters.

SELECT TREATISES OF ST. ATHANASIUS IN CONTROVERSY WITH THE ARIANS. Freely Translated.
Two vols. Crown 8vo. 7s.

First published in 1881. The first volume contains the "Treatises"; the second the notes alphabetically arranged so as to form a kind of theological lexicon to St. Athanasius's writings.

In 1842 Newman contributed to the Oxford Library of the Fathers two volumes entitled *Select Treatises of St. Athanasius in Controversy with the Arians.* This work was described by the late Canon Bright as ranking "among the richest treasures of English Patristic literature"; by the late Canon Liddon as "the most important contribution to the Library"; and in later prospectuses of the Library, after Newman's connection with it had ceased, as "the most important work published since Bishop Bull". The present edition differs from that of the Oxford Library in four important points, viz.: (1) the freedom of the translation; (2) the arrangement of the notes; (3) the omission of the fourth "Discourse against the Arians"; (4) the omission of some lengthy Dissertations. A Latin version of these last is included in *Tracts: Theological and Ecclesiastical.*

TRACTS: THEOLOGICAL and ECCLESIASTICAL.
Crown 8vo. 3s. 6d.

CONTENTS.—I. Dissertatiunculæ Quatuor Critico-Theologicæ [Rome 1847]—II. On the Text of the Epistles of St. Ignatius[1870]—III. Causes of the Rise and Success of Arianism [1872]—IV. The Heresy of Apollinaris—V. St. Cyril's Formula ΜΙΑ ΦΥΣΙΣ ΣΕΣΑΡΚΩ-ΜΕΝΗ. (*Atlantis*, 1858)—VI. The Ordo de Tempore in the Breviary. (*Atlantis*, 1870)— VII. History of the Text of the Douay Version of Scripture. (*Rambler*, 1859).

6. POLEMICAL.

THE VIA MEDIA OF THE ANGLICAN CHURCH.
Illustrated in Lectures, Letters and Tracts written between 1830 and 1841. Two vols. Crown 8vo. 3s. 6d. each.

This collection was first published in 1877.

CONTENTS OF VOL. I.—*The Prophetical Office of the Church, etc.,* originally published in 1837, reprinted with Notes and a Preface.

The Preface, which extends to about ninety pages, is one of Newman's most important polemical writings. His adversary is his former self. In his "Essay on Development," he dealt with one of the two great charges he used to bring against the Catholic Church; in this Preface he deals with the other.

CONTENTS OF VOL. II.—I. Suggestions in behalf of the Church Missionary Society, 1830 —II. Via Media, 1834 (being Nos. 38 and 40 of *Tracts for the Times*)—III. Restoration of Suffragan Bishops, 1835—IV. On the Mode of Conducting the Controversy with Rome (being No. 71 of *Tracts for the Times*)—V. Letter to a Magazine in behalf of Dr. Pusey's Tracts on Holy Baptism, 1837—VI. Letter to the Margaret Professor of Divinity on Mr. R. H. Froude's Statements on the Holy Eucharist, 1838—VII. Remarks on Certain Passages in the Thirty-nine Articles, 1841 (being No. 90 of *Tracts for the Times*)—VIII. Documentary Matter consequent upon the foregoing Remarks on the Thirty-nine Articles—IX. Letter to Dr. Jelf in Explanation of the Remarks, 1841—X. Letter to the Bishop of Oxford on the same Subject, 1841—XI. Retractation of Anti-Catholic Statements, 1843-45.

*** No. VII. in this Volume is the famous Tract 90 of *Tracts for the Times*, the whole with new Notes.

Cardinal Newman's Works—*continued.*

CERTAIN DIFFICULTIES FELT BY ANGLICANS
IN CATHOLIC TEACHING CONSIDERED.   Two vols.   Crown 8vo.   3s. 6d. each.

CONTENTS OF VOL. I.—Twelve Lectures addressed in 1850 to the party of the Religious Movement of 1833.

CONTENTS OF VOL. II.—I. Letter addressed to Rev. E. B. Pusey, D.D., on Occasion of his Eirenicon of 1864—II. A Letter addressed to the Duke of Norfolk, on Occasion of Mr. Gladstone's Expostulation of 1874.

LECTURES ON THE PRESENT POSITION OF
CATHOLICS IN ENGLAND.   Addresses to the Brothers of the Oratory in the Summer of 1851.   Crown 8vo.   3s. 6d.

APOLOGIA PRO VITA SUA, being a History of his
Religious Opinions.

First published in 1864.

Crown 8vo.   3s. 6d.
Pocket Edition.   Fcp. 8vo.   Cloth, 2s. 6d. *net.*   Leather, 3s. 6d. *net.*
Popular Edition.   8vo.   Paper covers, 6d. *net.*

The " Pocket " Edition and the " Popular " Edition of this book contain a letter, hitherto unpublished, written by Cardinal Newman to Canon Flanagan in 1857, which may be said to contain in embryo the " Apologia " itself.

7. LITERARY.

LOSS AND GAIN : The Story of a Convert.   Cr. 8vo.   3s. 6d.

First published in 1848.

"Of his experience as a Catholic, *Loss and Gain*, published in 1848, was the first fruit . . . the book has been a great favourite with me, almost ever since its first publication, partly for the admirable fidelity with which it sketches young men's thoughts and difficulties, partly for its happy irony, partly for its perfect representation of the academical life and tone at Oxford. . . . In the course of the story there are many happy sketches of Oxford society, such as, for example, the sketch of the evangelical pietism which Mr. Freeborn pours forth at Bateman's breakfast, or the sketch of the Rev. Dr. Brownside's prim and pompous Broad Church University sermon. . . . Again, there is one very impressive passage *not* taken from Oxford life, in which Newman makes . . . [one of his characters] insist on the vast difference between the Protestant and Roman Catholic conception of worship."—R. H. HUTTON's *Cardinal Newman.*

CALLISTA : A Tale of the Third Century.   Cr. 8vo.   3s. 6d.

¹ First published in 1855, with postscripts of 1856, 1881, 1888.

"It is an attempt to imagine and express, from a Catholic point of view, the feelings and mutual relations of Christians and heathens at the period to which it belongs."

Author's Preface.

VERSES ON VARIOUS OCCASIONS.
Crown 8vo.   3s. 6d.
Pocket Edition.   Fcp. 8vo.   Gilt top, Cloth, 2s. *net.*   Leather, 3s. *net.*

THE DREAM OF GERONTIUS.
16mo.   Paper covers, 6d.   Cloth, 1s. *net.*

With Introduction and Notes by MAURICE FRANCIS EGAN, D.D., LL.D.   With Portrait.   Crown 8vo.   1s. 6d.

Presentation Edition, with an Introduction specially written for this Edition by E. B(L).   With Photogravure Portrait of Cardinal Newman, and 5 other Illustrations.   Large Crown 8vo.   Cream cloth, with gilt top, 3s. *net.*

LITERARY SELECTIONS FROM NEWMAN.   With
Introduction and Notes by A SISTER OF NOTRE DAME.
Crown 8vo.   1s. 6d.   (*Longmans' Class-Books of English Literature.*)

Cardinal Newman's Works—*continued.*

8. DEVOTIONAL.

MEDITATIONS AND DEVOTIONS. Part I. Meditations for the Month of May. Novena of St. Philip. Part II. The Stations of the Cross. Meditations and Intercessions for Good Friday. Litanies, etc. Part III. Meditations on Christian Doctrine. Conclusion. Crown 8vo. 5s. *net.*

Also in Three Parts as follows. Fcap. 8vo. Cloth, 1s. *net* each. Limp leather, 2s. *net* each.

Part I. THE MONTH OF MAY.

Part II. STATIONS OF THE CROSS.

Part III. MEDITATIONS ON CHRISTIAN DOCTRINE.

9. BIOGRAPHIES.

THE LIFE OF JOHN HENRY CARDINAL NEWMAN. Based on his Private Journals and Correspondence. By WILFRID WARD. With 2 Portraits. 2 vols. 8vo. 12s. 6d. *net.*

LETTERS AND CORRESPONDENCE OF JOHN HENRY NEWMAN DURING HIS LIFE IN THE ENGLISH CHURCH. With a brief Autobiography. Edited, at Cardinal Newman's request, by ANNE MOZLEY. 2 vols. Crown 8vo. 7s.

" Materials for the present work were placed in the Editor's hands towards the close of 1884. The selection from them was made, and the papers returned to Cardinal Newman in the summer of 1887."—*Editor's Note.*

" It has ever been a hobby of mine, though perhaps it is a truism, that the true life of a man is in his letters. . . . Not only for the interest of a biography, but for arriving at the inside of things, the publication of letters is the true method. Biographers varnish, they assign motives, they conjecture feelings, they interpret Lord Burleigh's nods; but contemporary letters are facts."—*Dr. Newman to his sister, Mrs. John Mozley, May 18, 1863.*

10. POSTHUMOUS.

ADDRESSES TO CARDINAL NEWMAN, WITH HIS REPLIES, 1879-81. Edited by the Rev. W. P. NEVILLE (Cong. Orat.). With Portrait Group. Oblong crown 8vo. 6s. *net.*

NEWMAN MEMORIAL SERMONS: Preached at the Opening of the Newman Memorial Church, The Oratory, Birmingham, 8th and 12th December, 1909. By Rev. Fr. JOSEPH RICKABY, S.J., and Very Rev. Canon McINTYRE, Professor of Scripture at St. Mary's College, Oscott. 8vo. Paper covers, 1s. *net.*

SERMON NOTES, 1849-78. Edited by the FATHERS OF THE BIRMINGHAM ORATORY. With Portrait. Crown 8vo. 5s. *net.*

Cardinal Newman left behind him two MS. volumes filled with notes or memoranda of Sermons and Catechetical Instructions delivered by him during the years 1847 to 1879.

Besides their utility to priests and teachers, it is hoped that the notes will appeal to all lovers of Newman's writings. So characteristic of him are they, in spite of their brevity, that their authorship would be at once recognised even if they appeared without his name. Those of an earlier date are specially interesting. They introduce the reader to Newman in the first days of his Catholic life, settling down to the ordinary duties of an English priest, and instructing a " Mixed Congregation " in the rudiments of Catholic Doctrine.

INDEX.

CPSIA information can be obtained at www.ICGtesting.com
Printed in the USA
LVOW101801131212

311549LV00025B/1507/P